THE VOCAL CONCERTOS

RECENT RESEARCHES IN THE MUSIC OF THE BAROQUE ERA

Robert L. Marshall, general editor

A-R Editions, Inc., publishes six quarterly series—

Recent Researches in the Music of the Middle Ages and Early Renaissance
Margaret Bent, general editor

Recent Researches in the Music of the Renaissance
James Haar, general editor

Recent Researches in the Music of the Baroque Era
Robert L. Marshall, general editor

Recent Researches in the Music of the Classical Era
Eugene K. Wolf, general editor

Recent Researches in the Music of the Nineteenth and Early Twentieth Centuries
Rufus Hallmark, general editor

Recent Researches in American Music
H. Wiley Hitchcock, general editor—

which make public music that is being brought to light
in the course of current musicological research.

Each volume in the *Recent Researches* is devoted
to works by a single composer or to a single genre of composition,
chosen because of its potential interest to scholars and performers,
and prepared for publication according to the standards that govern
the making of all reliable historical editions.

Subscribers to this series, as well as patrons of subscribing institutions,
are invited to apply for information about the "Copyright-Sharing Policy"
of A-R Editions, Inc., under which the contents of this volume
may be reproduced free of charge for study or performance.

Correspondence should be addressed:

A-R EDITIONS, INC.
315 West Gorham Street
Madison, Wisconsin 53703

RECENT RESEARCHES IN THE MUSIC OF THE BAROQUE ERA • VOLUMES LIV and LV

Gregor Aichinger

THE VOCAL CONCERTOS

Edited by William E. Hettrick

A-R EDITIONS, INC. • MADISON

To the memory of
Robert Austin Warner

Library of Congress Cataloging-in-Publication Data

Aichinger, Gregor, 1564–1628.
   [Vocal music.   Selections]
   The vocal concertos.

   1 score.
   (Recent researches in the music of the Baroque Era,
ISSN 0484–0828 ; v. 54–55)
   Sacred works for 2–5 voices and continuo.
   Figured bass realized for keyboard instrument.
   Words also printed as text with English translations on p.
   Includes bibliographical references.
   1. Sacred vocal ensembles with continuo—Scores.
I. Hettrick, William E.   II. Title.   III. Series.
M2.R238   vol. 54–55   [M2019.3]   86–752289
ISBN 0–89579–213–3

Contents

Concertos for Larger Ensembles

Preface

Introduction

The sacred concerto for small vocal ensemble and organ first appeared in print in Italian publications: Gabriele Fattorini's *I sacri concerti a due voci* (Venice, 1600 and 1602) and the *Cento concerti ecclesiastici* for one, two, three, and four voices (book 1: Venice, 1602) of Lodovico Grossi da Viadana. These few-voiced *concerti* were characterized by a separate thorough-bass part and, in the voice parts, by a new and distinctive texture, featuring (as Manfred Bukofzer has described it) "open work" or "*concertato* interplay."[1] This musical style became very popular during the first half of the seventeenth century, not only in Italy but also in Germany,[2] where Viadana's works began to be reprinted in Frankfurt in 1609, and where, already in 1607, Gregor Aichinger had published his *Cantiones ecclesiasticae* in Dillingen. Aichinger's collection—the earliest significant German publication of music with thorough-bass, and specifically of music in the style of Viadana's *concerti*—contains mostly works for three voices and organ. In a short treatise printed in the *Bassus generalis* (organ) partbook, Aichinger refers directly to Viadana and gives instructions on performance in words that are very similar to those used by the Italian composer in his own collection. Aichinger's treatise is quoted in full and compared to Viadana's in my critical edition of the *Cantiones ecclesiasticae* (Recent Researches in the Music the Baroque Era, vol. 13),[3] which also includes biographical information about Aichinger (1564–1628), a discussion of his musical style and thorough-bass practice, and a documentation of the extent of Viadana's reputation in Germany as the inventor of the new musical style and even of the thorough-bass itself. The present double volume complements the *Cantiones ecclesiasticae* edition to make up a critical anthology of all of Aichinger's surviving works in the style of the sacred vocal concerto.

The Music of This Edition

Following the appearance of the *Cantiones ecclesiasticae* in 1607, Aichinger published thirteen new collections of music, eight of which were printed with a thorough-bass part for the organ. In some of these, as well as in a few of his individual compositions that were included in contemporary anthologies, the organ part is a *basso seguente*, mostly doubling the lowest-sounding notes of the ensemble, even when lower voices drop out. It is not surprising that the *basso seguente* accompanies Aichinger's music in traditional styles, such as the polyphonic motet and the more homophonic textures found in hymn settings and sacred canzonettas. (In this case the thorough-bass part serves the same function as a traditional organ intabulation, providing the organist with notation from which to play an accompaniment; in a sense, the organ intabulation must be considered superior, since it supplies much more information about the voices in the ensemble.) A second type of thorough-bass is also found in Aichinger's works, one that may be called "essentially independent." Although it may double the bass voice in the manner of a *basso seguente*, it provides an independent bass line whenever the vocal bass drops out momentarily or is absent altogether from the vocal ensemble in a given piece. Again not surprisingly, this essentially independent thorough-bass accompanies music cast in the progressive vein of the few-voiced *concertato*. Indeed, it is fundamental to the concerto style because it makes possible the open work and free interplay of the upper voices. The essentially independent thorough-bass is a distinguishing characteristic of the music in the present edition.[4]

Of Aichinger's eight collections of music with thorough-bass published after 1607, five contain music in concerto style and are therefore represented in this edition (see the lists of their contents under Sources). For the sake of completeness and continuity, all eight collections are described here.

A major source of Aichinger's early vocal concertos is unfortunately lost, as his *Cantiones* (1609)[5] survive today in only the Tenor and Bassus partbooks, and only six compositions from this collection can be salvaged from reprints in contemporary anthologies published by Johann Donfrid.[6] In these works the thorough-bass parts in the two- and three-voice pieces show considerable independence, even in the presence of a bass voice. This collection contains thirteen concertos for two voices (mostly combining a soprano with a lower voice), three for three voices, and four for four voices. Included also are five instrumental canzonas, one in four parts and four in five parts. Since the missing partbooks include the Octava pars, in which—according to the title page—the *Bassus generalis seu partitura* was to be found, it cannot be known if the canzonas also had a thorough-bass.

Aichinger next published collections of music with thorough-bass in 1615 (*Officium pro defunctis*, Augsburg) and 1616 (*Triplex liturgiarum fasciculus*, Augsburg). Both of these collections display traditional musical styles. Although the 1615 publication is now lost, it can be assumed that the original organ part was a *basso seguente*, since the music exists also in a manuscript version (in the Staats- und Stadtbibliothek, Augsburg) for voices only. The *Triplex liturgiarum fasciculus*, written for vocal ensembles ranging from four to six voices, contains three Masses, two of which are parody compositions based on Italian madrigals.

The contents of Aichinger's *Encomium* (1617) are all written for four voices and thorough-bass. The collection begins with two groups of hymn settings and ends with three Marian antiphons, of which the "Salve Regina" is a parody setting of Giovanni Gabrieli's eight-voice "Lieto godea" reduced to four voices. In these pieces the thorough-bass is fundamentally a *basso seguente*, although it does provide occasional independent notes by sustaining or anticipating the notes of the vocal bass. At any rate, Aichinger evidently considered it not essential to the performance of this music, for he specifically announces the beginning of "Angelus sanctae Gabriel Mariae" (included in this edition, no. [33]) in the Bassus partbook with the words *Hic requiritur necessariò Bassus generalis* ("here the thorough-bass is necessarily required"). Aichinger probably had this direction printed in the vocal bass part and not in the part to which it refers because he could not be sure that the *Bassus generalis* partbook would be used for all the compositions in the collection.

"Angelus sanctae Gabriel Mariae" is an interesting composition that deserves further discussion here. The text is an Annunciation hymn that Aichinger had set to music earlier, in his *Liber secundus sacrarum cantionum* (Venice, 1595). Although the source of the poem remains unidentified, its style is strongly reminiscent of the Latin poetry of Jacob Pontanus (Spanmüller), a Jesuit active in Augsburg in Aichinger's time.[7] Pontanus's verses are set to music elsewhere in the *Encomium* ("Hymnum canamus Virgini") and also in two of Aichinger's other collections. All five verses of Aichinger's *Encomium* setting of "Angelus sanctae Gabriel Mariae" are constructed on variants of the same bass line, which he identifies in the partbooks with the inscription *Sopra il aria ortensia*. His source was the "Aria della Signora Ortensia," which was published in a keyboard version in Marco Facoli's *Secondo libro d'intavolatura di balli* (Venice, 1588).[8] Facoli's piece consists of five phrases of four measures each, with the following notes predominating in the bass line:

    Phrase 1: G, C, F, D
    Phrase 2: B♭, F, G, D, G
    Phrase 3: B♭, E♭, B♭, F, B♭
    Phrase 4: B♭, G, F, G, C, D, G
    Phrase 5 ("Le Riprese"): C, D, G; C, D, G

Aichinger uses only the first four phrases as a model for the five verses of his setting, generally retaining the original order of the notes but composing freely around them, repeating sections, sometimes breaking up phrases or omitting them altogether, and occasionally adding whole sections not derived from the model. Thus, in his *Prima pars* bass line, mm. 1–4 are based on phrase 1, mm. 5–6 on phrase 2 (first half), mm. 7–9 on phrase 3 (omitting the F), mm. 9–14 on phrase 2 (stated twice, the first note eliding with the last note of phrase 3 in m. 9), mm. 15–20 on phrase 1 again, and mm. 20–27 on phrase 4 (stated twice). All four phrases of the model also appear in some form in each of the next three *partes*, but the *Quinta et ultima pars* is incomplete in this regard, containing only phrase 1 (mm. 1–11), phrase 4 (mm. 17–19 and 25–28), and material possibly derived from the second half of phrase 2 (mm. 12–16 and 20–24).

Also published in 1617, Aichinger's *Officium Angeli custodis* (Ingolstadt) contains settings for four voices of liturgical texts from First and Second Vespers and the Proper of the Mass in the Feast of the Holy Guardian Angels, in addition to the Litany of the Angels. A thorough-bass part (essentially of the *basso seguente* type) is included only in the compositions that are not based on plainchant *cantus firmi*: traditional, motet-style settings of the Hymn at Vespers; the Gradual, Alleluia, and Offertory at Mass; and the Litany.

In both *Quercus* (1619) and *Corolla* (1621), a preference can be seen on Aichinger's part for writing two equal voices, usually sopranos or tenors, with or without a bass voice. In most cases tenors are given as alternates for sopranos, and vice versa. Alto voices are used only occasionally in Aichinger's smaller vocal ensembles, and basses generally go along with the thorough-bass. In fact, the customary interdependence between vocal and instrumental bass parts in music of this period is illustrated in a revealing way in Aichinger's "Caro mea," as presented in this edition (no. [7]). It appeared originally in *Corolla* as a piece for two tenors (or sopranos) with organ, but it was printed subsequently in Johann Donfrid's *Prompt. mus.* (RISM 1627[1]) with an added vocal bass part. Since it goes along in unison with the thorough-bass, this vocal bass part is similar to those written by Aichinger, but in several places both bass parts move together in parallel unisons or fifths with one of the tenor parts (fifths in m. 12; unisons in mm. 17–18, 23, 24, 48, 49–50, and 54). Unison doubling and even consecutive fifths between the thorough-bass and a vocal part are frequent enough in Aichinger's compositions to be considered a characteristic aspect of his style, but this kind of writing rarely involves a second voice, extending the parallel motion to two members of the vocal ensemble. It is therefore apparent on stylistic grounds that the vocal bass part in "Caro mea" did not originate with Aichinger, but was concocted out of his thorough-bass, probably by Johann Donfrid. The spurious bass part has been included in the present edition as an example of this interesting method of musical arrangement.

Normally, Aichinger's music with essentially independent thorough-bass is freely composed and not based on pre-existent musical material. Exceptions to this rule include his "Angelus sanctae Gabriel Mariae," described above, and his "Ecce Panis Angelorum," printed in *Corolla* (1621) (this edition, no. [9]). In this duet for two tenors (or sopranos) and organ, the vocal parts paraphrase the corresponding plainsong phrases of the text source, verse 21 of the sequence "Lauda Sion."[9] As in the case of Aichinger's other collections, the music from *Quercus* (1619) and *Corolla* (1621) not included in this edition has a thorough-bass that is a *basso seguente*. This includes a set of eight hymn settings (beginning with "Mater supraemi numinis") in *Corolla* written for two sopranos and bass, a vocal ensemble normally typical of Aichinger's works in the more progressive, concerto style.[10]

Flores (1626), Aichinger's last published collection of music, contains pieces for five or six voices and thorough-bass. In most of these compositions, including five *contrafacta* of Italian madrigals by Luca Marenzio and Orlando di Lasso, the thorough-bass functions as a *basso seguente* and the musical style is conservative; but an essentially independent thorough-bass characterizes two substantial works from the collection that are included in this edition, "Angelus Domini descendit" (no. [34]) and "Paratum cor meum" (no. [35]). These remarkable pieces are unique among Aichinger's surviving compositions: first, he calls them "concertos," his only known use of that term in his music; second, they combine three voices and organ with an additional ensemble of two violins. Both concertos include solos for individual voices, interludes for violins, and other combinations of vocal and instrumental forces. They are written in a style that anticipates the music of Andreas Hammerschmidt and Heinrich Schütz. Although the Quintus partbook of *Flores* (1626) does not survive, it has been possible to supply an editorial second violin part through a careful analysis of the musical context.

Sources

The following inventory comprises all of the extant printed collections containing works presented in this edition. (There are no original manuscript sources of this music.) This inventory is not meant to be a complete catalogue of all of Aichinger's compositions, or even all of them with thorough-bass. The list is presented in two parts, each organized chronologically according to publication date. In the first part, listing Aichinger's own printed collections, all of the contents are given; for contemporary anthologies compiled by others, listed in the second part, only the pieces by Aichinger are given. In both parts each concerto included in the present edition is identified by an asterisk printed before the title. Numbers given here follow the enumeration in the sources in question, except for those enclosed in square brackets, which are editorial.

For Aichinger's own collections, all known present locations of partbooks are given and are identified by means of the RISM sigla listed below. All of these copies, complete or otherwise, have been employed in the preparation of this edition. For the other collections, however, only one copy of each has been consulted; the locations of these copies are likewise identified. The editor hereby expresses his gratitude to the directors of the following libraries, who kindly permitted their holdings to be consulted for the present edition:

A—Austria

A: Wn	Vienna, Österreichische Nationalbibliothek, Musiksammlung

D-brd—Federal Republic of Germany

D-brd: As	Augsburg, Staats- und Stadtbibliothek
D-brd: F	Frankfurt, Stadt- und Universitätsbibliothek
D-brd: Hs	Hamburg, Staats- und Universitätsbibliothek, Musikabteilung
D-brd: Mbs	Munich, Bayerische Staatsbibliothek, Musiksammlung
D-brd: Rp	Regensburg, Proskesche Musikbibliothek (Bischöfliche Zentralbibliothek)

F—France

F: Pn	Paris, Bibliothèque Nationale, Département de la musique

GB—Great Britain

GB: Lbm	London, British Library, Music Library

In all of the designations of parts in the following inventory (and in Texts, Translations, and Commentary), the presence of thorough-bass (Bassus generalis or Partitura) is to be understood; possible exceptions are the five canzonas (nos. 36–40) in the *Cantiones* (1609), which may not have included thorough-bass. Where a slash separates two voice indications (e.g., "C/T"), the second is an alternative given in the original source. The abbreviations used here to identify partbooks or individual parts are the following: C = Cantus; A = Altus; T = Tenor; B = Bassus; and Bg = Bassus generalis.

Aichinger's Own Printed Collections

CANTIONES (1609)

Altera pars huius operis [referring to *Sacrae Dei laudes* (Dillingen: Adam Meltzer, 1609), of which this is a continuation]. *Cantiones nimirum 2. 3. 4. 5. vocum, una cum basso generali seu partitura ad organum, quam invenies in octava parte* (Dillingen: Adam Meltzer, 1609)

Incomplete: D-brd: As (T), Mbs (T, B)

16.   Decantabat populus Israel (C, B)
17.   *Mirabile mysterium (C, B)
18.   *Angelus Domini (C, B)
19.   Sicut Mater (C, C)
20.   Congratulamini mihi omnes (C, T)
21.   Angelus ad pastores ait (C, T)
22.   Pastores loquebantur (C, T)
23.   Dies sanctificatus (C, T)
24.   Exaudi Deus (C, A)
25.   *Adorna thalamum tuum (A, A)
26.   Omni tempore benedic Deum (A, B)
27.   Unam petii a Domino (T, T)
28.   Usti sunt agni novelli (T, T)
29.   Verbum caro factum est (C, C, B)
30.   *Et vidi, et ecce (T, T, T)
31.   *Deus meus (T, B, B)
32.   *Quem terra, pontus, aethera (C, A, T, B)
33.   Tibi Christe (C, C, B, B)
34.   Exurgat Deus (T, T, B, B)
35.   Domus mea (T, T, B, B)
36.   Canzon per sonare il primo (C, C, B, B)
37.   Canzon per sonare il secondo (*a 5*)
38.   Canzon per sonare il tertio (*a 5*)
39.   Canzon per sonare il quarto (*a 5*)
40.   Canzon per sonare il quinto (*a 5*)

ENCOMIUM (1617)

Encomium verbo incarnato, eiusdemque Matri augustissimae Reginae caelorum musicis numeris decantatum (Ingolstadt: Gregor Hänlin, 1617)

D-brd: Mbs (Bg), Rp (C, A, T, B, Bg)

[1]   Verbum caro factum est (6 *partes*) (C, A, T, B)
[2]   Hymnum canamus Virgini (7 *partes*) (C, C, A, B)
[3]   *Angelus sanctae Gabriel Mariae (5 *partes*) (C, C, T, B)
[4]   Alma Redemptoris Mater (C, C, A, B)
[5]   Ave Regina caelorum (C, A, T, B)
[6]   Salve, Regina (C, A, T, B)

QUERCUS (1619)

Quercus Dodonaea cuius vocales glandes suavitate cycnea saporatas, olorina canitie nitentes in sacro Jovi musisą; nemore decussit & legit, ac trimodio seu triodia est admensus (Augsburg: Johann Praetorius, 1619)

D-brd: Hs (C2)[11], Rp (C1, C2, B, Bg)

1. *Regi saeculorum immortali (C/T, C/T, B)
2. *Nativitas tua (C/T, C/T, B)
3. *O beata ubera (C/T, C/T, B)
4. *Salve, Regina (*prima pars*) (C/T, C/T, B)
5. *Et Jesum benedictum fructum (*secunda pars*) (C/T, C/T, B)
6. *Beatus vir (C/T, C/T, B)
7. *Laetamini in Domino (C/T, C/T, B)
8. *Media nocte (C/T, C/T, A/B)
9. *In omnem terram (C/T, C/T, B)
10. *Jesu nostra redemptio (C/T, C/T, B)
11. *Ave Regina caelorum (A, T, B)
12. *Justus ut palma florebit (T, T, B)
13. *Ecce sacerdos magnus (T, T, B)
14. *Hoc in templo (C, C, A)
15. Ecce quam bonum (C, A, T, B)

COROLLA (1621)

Corolla eucharistica, ex variis flosculis et gemmulis pretiosis musarum sacrarum, binis ternisą; vocibus contexta. Cui etiam aeternae Virginis uniones quidam de Tessera salutis affixi (Augsburg: Johann Praetorius, 1621)

D-brd: F (T1), Rp (T1, T2, B, Bg)

1. *Hic est panis (T/C, T/C)
2. *Domine, non sum dignus (T/C, T/C)
3. *Discubuit Jesus (T/C, T/C)
4. *Caro mea (T/C, T/C)
5. *Amen, amen dico vobis (T/C, T/C)
6. *Ecce Panis Angelorum (T/C, T/C)
7. *Adoro te supplex (T/C, T/C)
8. *Ave, vivens hostia (C/T, C/T, B)
9. *Memoriam fecit (C/T, C/T, B)
10. *O sacrum convivium! (C/T, C/T, T)
11. Jesu mi bone sentiam (C/T, C/T, B)
12. Jam quod quaesivi (C/T, C/T, B)
13. Mater supraemi numinis (*prima pars*) (C, C, B)
14. Te Virgo nil formosius (*secunda pars*) (C, C, B)
15. Hestera pulchritudine (*tertia pars*) (C, C, B)
16. Tu castitatis lilium (*quarta pars*) (C, C, B)
17. Opem tuam qui flagitat (*quinta pars*) (C, C, B)
18. Seu tentet omnes machinas (*sexta pars*) (C, C, B)
19. Seu faeda flamma cypridos (*septima pars*) (C, C, B)
20. O magna Mater numinis (*octava pars*) (C, C, B)
21. *Regina caeli laetare (T/C, T/C)

FLORES (1626)

Flores musici ad mensam SS. convivii quinque & sex vocibus concinendi, & in xenium praeparati dicatiáque, Reverendissimo in Christo P. Dno. Dn Joanni, incliti monasterii ad SS. Udalricum & Afram praesuli, &c. (Augsburg: Johann Ulrich Schönigk, for Caspar Flurschütz, 1626)

Incomplete: A: Wn (Partitura); D-brd: Rp (C, A, T, B)

1. O vere digna hostia (C, C, A, T, B)
2. Haec esca laethum efficit (C, C, A, T, B)
3. Jesu mi bone sentiam (C, C, A, T, B)

4. Verbum supernum prodiens (C, C, A, T, B)
5. Desidero te millies (C, C, A, T, B)
6. O Jesu mi dulcissime (C, C, A, T, B)
7. Amor Jesu dulcissimus (C, C, A, T, B)
8. Tantum ergo Sacramentum (C, C, A, T, B)
9. Adoro te supplex (C, C, A, T, B)
10. Ave verbum incarnatum (C, C, A, T, B)
11. *Angelus Domini descendit (Violino, Violino, C, T, B)
12. *Paratum cor meum (Violino, Violino, C, T, B)
13. Ecce Panis Angelorum (2 *partes*) (C, C, A, T, T, B)
14. Anima Christi sanctifica me (3 *partes*) (C, C, A, T, T, B)
15. O salutaris hostia (2 *partes*) (C, C, A, T, T, B)
16. O quam suavis est Dominus (C, C, A, T, T, B)
17. Sacerdos in aeternum (C, A, T, T, T, B)
18. Media vita in morte sumus (C, C, A, T, T, B)
19. Sacrosancte individuae Trinitati (C, C, A, T, T, B)

Anthologies

SIREN (RISM 1616[2])

Georg Victorinus, *Siren coelestis duarum, trium et quatuor vocum, quam novavit e principibus, etiam nec dum vulgatis auctoribus legit, pro temporum dierumque, festorum diversitate concinnavit, organis item accommodavit, et in lucem dedit* (Munich: Adam Berg, 1616)

D-brd: Rp

44. *Duo Seraphim (C/T, C/T, A)

SIREN (RISM 1622[3])

Georg Victorinus, *Siren coelestis centum harmoniarum duarum, trium et quatuor vocum, quam novavit e principibus, etiam nec dum vulgatis auctoribus legit . . . Editio altera correctior & melior* (Munich: The Widow Berg, for Johann Hertsroy, 1622)

D-brd: F

44. *Duo Seraphim (C/T, C/T, A)

PROMPT. MUS. (RISM 1622[2])

Johann Donfrid, *Promptuarii musici, concentus ecclesiasticos II. III. et IV. vocum cum basso continuo & generali, organo applicato, e diversis, iisque illustrissimis et musica laude praestantissimis hujus aetatis autoribus, collectos exhibentis. Pars prima* (Strassburg: Paul Ledertz, 1622)

F: Pn

8. *Angelus Domini (C, B)
41. *Mirabile mysterium (C, B)
98. *Et vidi, et ecce (T, T, T)
127. *Adorna thalamum tuum (A, A)
159. *Deus meus (T, B, B)

PROMPT. MUS. (RISM 1623[2])

Johann Donfrid, *Promptuarii musici concentus, ecclesiasticos ducentos et eo amplius. II. III. & IV. vocum. Cum basso continuo & generali, organo applicato, e diversis, iisque clarissimis et musica laude praestantissimis, hujus aetatis autoribus, collectos exhibentis. Pars altera* (Strassburg: Paul Ledertz, 1623)

F: Pn

136. *Duo Seraphim (C/T, C/T, A)
146. Tres sunt (A, T, B)

PHILOMELA (RISM 1624[1])

Georg Victorinus, *Philomela coelestis. Sive suavissimae lectissimaeque cantiones sacrae cum falsabordonis, magnificat, canzonis, & basso ad organum, duarum, trium, & quatuor vocum, antè hac nec auditae, nec divulgatae* (Munich: Nicolaus Henricus, for Georg Victorinus, 1624)

D-brd: Mbs (vox suprema, vox media, vox infima); GB: Lbm (Bg)

41. *In nomine Jesu (C, C, B)

PROMPT. MUS. (RISM 1627[1])

Johann Donfrid, *Promptuarii musici, concentus ecclesiasticos CCLXXXVI. selectissimos, II. III. & IV. vocum. Cum basso continuo & generali, organo applicato, e diversis et praestantissimis Germaniae Italiae & aliis aliarum terrarum musicis collectos exhibens, pars tertia* (Strassburg: Paul Ledertz, 1627)

F: Pn

109. *Caro mea (T, T, B)
205. *Nativitas tua (C/T, C/T, B)

VIRIDARIUM (RISM 1627[2])

Johann Donfrid, *Viridarium musico Marianum. Concentus ecclesiasticos plus quam ducentos, in dialogo, II. III. & IV. vocum, cum basso continuo & generali, organo applicato, e diversis iisque clarissimis et musica laude praestantissimis hujus aetatis autoribus, pro omni genere & sorte cantorum, summa diligentia collectos* (Strassburg: Lazarus Zetzner's Heirs, 1627)

F: Pn

46. *Regina caeli laetare (T/C, T/C)
95. *O beata ubera (C/T, C/T, B)
115. *Ave Regina caelorum (A, T, B)
164. *Congratulamini mihi omnes (C, A, T, B)
185. *Quem terra, pontus, aethera (C, A, T, B)

Editorial Procedures

In the present edition each vocal or instrumental part in each concerto is based on one primary source, always the earliest one extant. In most cases the earliest sources are Aichinger's own printed collections; exceptions to this rule have been necessary only in editing the six pieces from the incompletely preserved *Cantiones* (1609) (nos. [1], [2], [3], [12], [13], and [32]) and, of course, for the two pieces not printed in Aichinger's collections (nos. [14] and [31]).

In this edition, all material enclosed in square brackets or printed as small notes (for example, the thorough-bass realization) has been added by the editor to the reading presented in the primary source. Additional editorial procedures are described below.

Music

The editorial incipit provided for each part at the beginning of each piece gives the following information about that part as it appears in the primary source: clef, key signature, first note (or notes, in the case of a ligature), and name (either as given explicitly or as implied by the clef). Initial rests are not shown in the incipit. Part

names in parentheses represent alternate octave transpositions indicated in the sources. An editorial indication of the range of each voice part (and of the violin parts in nos. [34] and [35]) is also provided.

Accidentals appearing in the sources are presented in their modern forms in the musical notation of this edition, and all sharps used originally as cancellation signs are rendered here as naturals. Accidentals enclosed here in square brackets are editorial additions that represent changes from the original notation not already described above. Accidentals enclosed in parentheses are editorial marks that clarify the meaning of the original notation; they function here as cautionary or cancellation signs that reaffirm the key signature. In the notation of this edition, any accidental (not belonging to the key signature), once presented in a part, prevails in that part until it is cancelled by a solid or broken barline or by a different accidental in the same part affecting the same note. (For an explanation of the broken barline, see under Thorough-Bass below.) The status of the accidental in question (that is, whether it is original or added by the editor) also carries through until it is cancelled by one of the symbols listed above or by a repetition of the same accidental with a different status. Cautionary accidentals in the sources, which served to keep B-naturals (or E-naturals, when B-flat is in the key signature) from being lowered in performance through the application of *musica ficta* but are not necessary in modern practice, are indicated here only in the Commentary. Accidentals in the thorough-bass figuration are discussed below.

Original note values in duple meters are reduced to one-half in the present edition; in triple meters the note values are reduced to one-quarter throughout. All final notes are given here with fermatas and with the note values of a full measure in the modern notation, regardless of their values and the presence or absence of fermatas in the original. Ligatures and coloration are indicated, respectively, by the symbols ⌐⌐ and ⌐ ⌐ .

Text

All texts set to music in Aichinger's concertos have been made, in this edition, to conform to the standards of spelling, capitalization, punctuation, and syllabification found in the *Biblia sacra* (the Vulgate), the *Liber usualis*, and other official liturgical publications of the Roman Catholic Church.

In rendering abbreviations used in the primary sources, the editor has adopted the following procedures: where symbols in the original stand for specific letters or words, they are written out in full here (e.g., "cū" becomes "cum"; "&" becomes "et"); however, where abbreviations in the sources present only portions of words, the portions there omitted are enclosed here in square brackets (e.g., "all." becomes "all[eluia]"). Words enclosed here in angled brackets, ⟨ ⟩, are repetitions indicated in the primary source by the symbol *ij* (appearing also as *ii*). In this edition no special mention is made of the several places in which more than one *ij* is used to show a single repetition of a phrase of text. In such cases, each additional appearance of the symbol served to indicate not a new repetition of a group of words, but merely the continuation of the initial repetition. However, every *ij* that is truly superfluous, not corresponding to any word or phrase of text, is reported in the Commentary. Likewise, all repetitions of text not originally indicated in any way are printed here within square brackets.

The editor has followed the primary sources as closely as possible in the matter of text underlay; nevertheless, at the few places where the original text is inconsistent, the most suitable distribution of the text has been chosen in accordance with the practices of the period. The positioning of syllables of text enclosed in brackets—either square or angled—is, of course, entirely editorial.

Thorough-Bass

With the advent of thorough-bass notation came a new meaning of accidentals in addition to their traditional function of altering the notes to which they were attached: they could now also indicate the chromatic inflection of notes a third (or, rarely, a sixth) above the notated bass line. At the time when Aichinger's concertos were originally printed, the positioning of these two types of accidentals was not standardized. Printers of the sixteenth and early seventeenth centuries frequently placed the first, traditional type directly above or below the note in question, evidently in order to save horizontal space. On the other hand, there are also examples of figuration accidentals (the second type) placed at the left of the notes in the bass line, usually on the same horizontal level, but occasionally on higher or lower levels. When the higher levels are consistently a third above the given notes, it may be concluded that the printer followed a definite, logical plan. But, for the most part, printers seem to have been concerned only with positioning accidentals as close as possible to their corresponding notes, using whatever typographical means they had available. Performers were evidently expected to distinguish between traditional and figuration accidentals according to the musical context. The addition of numbers to thorough-bass figuration added further complication. Frequently the number 6 was combined with a bass note that was chromatically raised, thus making a total of three symbols that were to be combined: the number, the accidental, and the note itself. Although many combinations were possible, Aichinger's printers tended to favor three, in vertical placement (reading from the top down): accidental, number, note; number, accidental, note; and number, note, accidental. In addition, the more modern placement of the accidental at the left of the note and the number above the note was also employed. Since little

significance can be observed in what seems to have been a haphazard practice, the present edition, while indicating all of the symbols in the thorough-bass, makes no attempt to show their original configuration. Where the original contains two consecutive notes of the same pitch with one figuration accidental placed in between (and usually above), this edition places the accidental under the first note. Aichinger's thorough-bass figuration is, of course, incomplete by later standards. However, nothing has been added here, except for an occasional "6" (enclosed in square brackets) necessary to show the function of a figuration sharp inflecting that interval, instead of the third, above the bass.

Most of the sources of Aichinger's concertos contain barlines in the notation of the thorough-bass part that divide the music into regular metrical units; these divisions are retained in the present edition (and extended to the upper vocal and instrumental parts) without notice. In this context, the occasional absence of a barline in the primary source is shown here in one of two ways: either by a broken barline or, if the absence occurs at the end of a staff in the original (which itself provides a delineation), by a solid barline with a small diagonal slash (†). Where thorough-bass barlines are mostly or completely absent in a source, this fact is reported in the Commentary. If the source is primary, then the thorough-bass barlines supplied here are editorial, and in this context both solid and broken barlines are used (the latter indicating the beginning of occasional incomplete measures).

Clef changes in the original notation of the thorough-bass part (usually associated with the doubling of higher voices in the manner of a *basso seguente*) are reported here in the Commentary.

Acknowledgments

This edition was prepared with the support and assistance of the following, to whom thanks are hereby expressed: the National Endowment for the Humanities, for a Summer Stipend for bibliographical research in Austria, Germany, and Italy; Hofstra University, for a sabbatical leave that allowed the bulk of the work on the edition to be completed; the Faculty Research and Development Fund of Hofstra College of Liberal Arts and Sciences, for financial help in acquiring some of the necessary sources on microfilm; and Prof. Margaret Schatkin, Department of Theology, Boston College, for her expert advice on the translation of several Latin texts.

William E. Hettrick

Notes

1. Manfred F. Bukofzer, *Music in the Baroque Era* (New York: W. W. Norton & Company, Inc., 1947), p. 66.

2. The extent of this style's popularity in both countries is documented and discussed in Adam Adrio, *Die Anfänge des geistlichen Konzerts* (Berlin: Junker und Dünnhaupt Verlag, 1935); and Anne Kirwan-Mott, *The Small-Scale Sacred Concertato in the Early Seventeenth Century*, 2 vols., Studies in British Musicology (Ann Arbor: UMI Research Press, 1981). Kirwan-Mott includes transcriptions of the following works by Aichinger (with the thorough-bass left unrealized) in her second volume: "Dixit Isaac patri suo" and "Ubi est Abel" from the *Cantiones ecclesiasticae* (1607); and "Duo Seraphim" (this edition, no. [14]).

3. Madison: A-R Editions, Inc., 1972. An additional source of some of the music in the *Cantiones ecclesiasticae* must be reported here: Ms. F. K. Musik No. 1 of the Fürstlich Thurn und Taxissche Hofbibliothek in Regensburg. This manuscript, written in mensural notation, contains (on pp. 1–21) the Cantus I part of Aichinger's seven Magnificats (nos. 2, 4, 6, 8, 10, 12, and 14 in the collection), most likely originally copied from the publication.

4. The subject of Aichinger's musical style as related to the function of his thorough-bass parts is treated extensively in my dissertation, *The Thorough-Bass in the Works of Gregor Aichinger (1564–1628)* (Ph.D. diss., University of Michigan, 1968), University Microfilms order no. 69–12, 132. This study also contains a complete inventory and discussion of the contents of all of Aichinger's printed collections of music with thorough-bass.

5. Aichinger's collections containing music included in the present edition are referred to here by sigla used in Sources, where additional bibliographical information is given.

6. The important work of this German compiler of sacred vocal music is discussed in Rainer Schmitt, *Untersuchungen zu Johann Donfrids Sammeldrucken unter besonderer Berücksichtigung der geistlichen Konzerte Urban Loths* (Ph.D. diss., Rheinische Friedrich-Wilhelms-Universität, Bonn, 1974).

7. Thanks are due to Dr. Renata Wagner of the Bayerische Staatsbibliothek, Munich, for her report that the text in question does not appear in Pontanus's *Parthenometricha, id est meditationes, preces, laudes in Virginem Matrem* (Augsburg, 1606), which seemed a likely source.

8. This collection has been edited by Willi Apel in Facoli's *Collected Works*, Corpus of Early Keyboard Music, vol. 2 (Dallas: American Institute of Musicology, 1963). I wish to acknowledge the help of the late John Reeves White, who identified the "aria ortensia" and called my attention to this source.

9. See the *Liber usualis*, ed. by the Benedictines of Solesmes (Tournai: Desclée & Co., 1961), p. 948.

10. These eight settings, called, collectively, *Hymnus Deiparae Virginis*, have been edited by Eberhard Kraus in Musik der Oberpfalz, vol. 2 (Regensburg: Bosse Edition, 1972).

11. *Signatur:* 9 an Scrin A/605.

Texts, Translations, and Commentary

Aichinger's concertos are listed here in the order in which they are presented in this edition. In the identification of each text, biblical references are given priority, even though the text in question may also appear in the liturgy; however, if a text is a composite of biblical passages but appears intact in the liturgy, the appropriate liturgical reference is given. References to the Psalms and to the book of John cite both Catholic and Protestant numberings, giving the latter in parentheses. Some of the texts set to music by Aichinger differ in certain respects from the corresponding biblical or liturgical sources; they are indicated here as altered. Translations given here are based on the Rheims-Douay Bible and, for certain liturgical texts, *The Hours of the Divine Office in English and Latin* (Collegeville, Minn.: The Liturgical Press, 1963).

Each source is identified by printed collection (using the abbreviations employed above in Sources) and number within that collection. If a source is incomplete, the surviving parts are also listed.

The Commentary contains information on variant readings and other aspects of the sources not indicated in the notation of this edition. Most items are identified by means of measure, staff, and note numbers, using the abbreviations listed below. Whenever a primary or secondary source needs to be specifically identified, collections are cited simply by the last two numerals in their dates: e.g., *Cantiones* (1609) becomes '09, and *Prompt. mus.* (RISM 1622²) becomes '22. Unless otherwise indicated, a reference to a given collection describes all of the copies of that collection consulted for this edition. All text cited in the Commentary is printed in italics. Pitches are designated according to the traditional system, with c' indicating middle C, etc. The following abbreviations are used in the Commentary: M. = measure; s. = staff (counting from the top of each system); ed. = edition; fig. = (thorough-bass) figuration; thr. = through; sig. = signature; C = Cantus; A = Altus; T = Tenor; B = Bassus; Bg = Bassus generalis.

[1] Mirabile mysterium

TEXT: Antiphon at Benediction at Lauds, the Circumcision of Our Lord (the Octave of the Nativity of Our Lord)

Mirabile mysterium declaratur hodie: innovantur naturae, Deus homo factus est: id quod fuit permansit, et quod non erat assumpsit; non commixtionem passus, nec divisionem. Alleluia.	A wondrous mystery is revealed this day: natures are renewed, God has become man. He remained what he was and assumed what he was not, undergoing neither confusion nor division. Alleluia.

SOURCES: *Cantiones* (1609), 17 (B only)
  Prompt. Mus. (RISM 1622²), 41

COMMENTARY: S. 4, no barlines in '22.
  M. 14, s. 2, note 3 (thr. m. 16, note 1), *natura* in '09. M. 33, s. 2, note 2 (thr. m. 34), *commistionem* in '09. M. 34, s. 2, notes 3–4, two semiminims incorrectly beamed together (making two fusas) by hand in '09. M. 44, s. 2, note 4, the ♯ for this note is printed at the left of the next note in '09. M. 45, s. 2, note 6 (thr. m. 47, note 1), *alleluia, alleluia* in '22. M. 46, s. 1, note 6 (thr. m. 47, note 1), *-luia* in '22. M. 49, s. 2, *alleluia* in '09 and '22. M. 50, s. 2, note 1, *alleluia* begins here in '22, with the last three syllables on m. 50, notes 4–5, and m. 51, note 1, respectively. M. 68, s. 2, note 3 (thr. m. 70, note 2), *commistionem* in '09 and '22. M. 80, s. 2, notes 2–3, '09 has first two syllables of an extra *alleluia* here, with the last two syllables on m. 81, notes 2–3. M. 81, s. 2, notes 2–4, *alleluia* given for these three notes in '22. M. 82, s. 2, note 3 (thr. m. 83, note 1), *alleluia* in '09. M. 83, s. 2, note 2, *ij* begins here in '09. M. 84, s. 2, note 2 (thr. m. 85, note 1), *alleluia* in '22. M. 85, s. 2, note 2, *ij* in '22. Mm. 86–87, s. 2, extra *alleluia* in '22.

[2] Angelus Domini

TEXT: Combination of Antiphon at Benediction at Lauds, Monday in First Week of Advent; Antiphon at Magnificat at Vespers, Wednesday in Third Week of Advent (Luke 1:38); and Responsory and Versicle in Terce, Nativity of Our Lord (John 1:14)

Angelus Domini annuntiavit Mariae, et concepit de Spiritu Sancto. Ecce ancilla Domini, fiat mihi secundum verbum tuum. Et verbum caro factum est, et habitavit in nobis. Alleluia.	The Angel of the Lord made the announcement to Mary, and she conceived by the Holy Spirit. "Behold the handmaiden of the Lord; let it be done unto me according to thy word." And the word was made flesh and dwelt among us. Alleluia.

SOURCES: *Cantiones* (1609), 18 (B only)
  Prompt. mus. (RISM 1622²), 8

COMMENTARY: S. 4, no barlines in '22.
  M. 1, s. 2, time sig. is ₡ in '22. M. 12, s. 4, note 6, g in '22. M. 18, s. 2, notes 2–5, text written out in '22. Mm. 50–52, s. 2, text written out in '22. Mm. 53–55, s. 2, text written out in '22. M. 58, s. 2, notes 1–4, text written out in '22. M. 58, s. 2, note 5 (thr. m. 59, note 1), *ij* in '22. M. 59, s. 2, note 6 (thr. m. 61, note 1), text written out in '22. M. 61, s. 2, note 2 (thr. m. 62, note 5), just one *alleluia* in '09 and one *ij* in '22. M. 62, s. 2, note 6 (thr. m.

63, note 2), text written out in '22.   M. 63, s. 2, note 3 (thr. m. 65), just one *ij* in '09 and one *alleluia* in '22.   M. 64, s. 4, note 6, c in '22.   Mm. 66–67, s. 2, *ij* in '22.

[3] Adorna thalamum tuum

TEXT: Responsory at Matins, Purification of the Blessed Virgin

Adorna thalamum tuum, Sion, et suscipe Regem Christum: quem virgo concepit, virgo peperit, virgo post partum, quem genuit, adoravit.	Adorn your bridal chamber, O Sion, and receive Christ the King. Whom the Virgin conceived, the Virgin brought forth; after childbirth, the Virgin adored him whom she bore.

SOURCES: *Cantiones* (1609), 25 (A only)
         Prompt. mus. (RISM 1622²), 127

COMMENTARY: S. 4, no barlines in '22.
    M. 9, s. 2, text written out in '22.   M. 18, s. 2, note 2, 2d syllable of *Christum* begins here in '22.   M. 33, s. 2, note 3 (thr. m. 34), text written out in '22.   M. 36, s. 2, note 2 (thr. m. 37, note 1), *ij* in '22.   M. 49, s. 2, note 3, ♯ lacking in '22.   M. 54, s. 2 (thr. m. 55, note 1), text written out in '22.   M. 55, s. 2, note 2 (thr. m. 56, note 1), *ij* in '22.

[4] Hic est panis

TEXT: John 6:59 (6:58)

Hic est panis qui de caelo descendit. Non sicut manducaverunt patres vestri manna, et mortui sunt. Qui manducat hunc panem, vivet in aeternum.	This is the bread that came down from heaven. Not as your fathers did eat manna, and are dead. He that eateth this bread shall live for ever.

SOURCE: *Corolla* (1621), 1

COMMENTARY: Mm. 19–21, s. 1 and 2, note use of black notation ("et mortui sunt").

[5] Domine, non sum dignus

TEXT: Spoken during Communion at Mass (derived from Matt. 8:8)

Domine, non sum dignus ut intres sub tectum meum: sed tantum dic verbo, et sanabitur anima mea.	Lord, I am not worthy that thou shouldst enter under my roof; but only say the word, and my soul shall be healed.

SOURCE: *Corolla* (1621), 2

COMMENTARY: M. 5, s. 4, note 2, fig. 6 placed over this note.   M. 15, s. 2, note 3, *die*.   M. 28, s. 2, note 5, minim.   M. 31, s. 1, note 2, dotted minim with head almost entirely black in D-brd: Rp copy.

[6] Discubuit Jesus

TEXT: Luke 22:14–15 (altered)

Discubuit Jesus cum discipulis suis. Et ait: Desiderio desideravi hoc pascha manducare vobiscum, antequam patiar.	Jesus sat with his disciples. And he said: "With desire I have desired to eat this pasch with you, before I suffer."

SOURCE: *Corolla* (1621), 3

COMMENTARY: M. 2, s. 4, after note 2, bass clef.   M. 29, s. 2, note 2, d' changed by hand (incorrectly) to c'.

[7] Caro mea

TEXT: John 6:56, 59 (6:56, 58)

Caro mea vere est cibus, et sanguis meus vere est potus. Qui manducat hunc panem, vivet in aeternum.	My flesh is meat indeed, and my blood is drink indeed. He that eateth this bread, shall live for ever.

SOURCES: *Corolla* (1621), 4
         Prompt. mus. (RISM 1627¹),109

COMMENTARY: T1 in vox secunda of '27, and T2 in vox prima; B found only in '27 (vox tertia).   T/C, T/C indicated in all parts in '21; T/C, T/C, B indicated in Bg of '27; and T, T, B indicated in remaining parts in '27.   S. 5, no barlines in '27, except as indicated below.
    M. 19, s. 1, note 1, cautionary ♯ in '21 and '27.   M. 21, s. 2, note 1, cautionary ♯ in '21 and '27.   M. 25, s. 2, text written out in '27.   M. 26, all parts, time sig. is **3** in '21 and '27.   M. 28, s. 1, note 1, cautionary ♯ in '21 and '27.   M. 34, s. 5, note 2, fig. ♯ lacking in '27.   M. 35, s. 1, note 1, cautionary ♯ in '21 and '27.   M. 38, s. 1, note 1, cautionary ♯ in '21 and '27.   M. 40, s. 2, note 2, cautionary ♯ in '21 and '27.   Mm. 43–45, s. 2, *ij* in '27.   M. 49, s. 5, note 2, F corrected by hand to d in '21.   M. 51, s. 5, e in '27.   M. 51, s. 5, barline after this measure (to ensure perfection of breve) in '27.   Mm. 52–58, s. 2, text written out in '27.   M. 53, s. 2, note 1, cautionary ♯ in '21 and '27.   M. 58, s. 5, barline after this measure (to ensure perfect breve) in '27.   Mm. 63–65, s. 2, text written out in '27. M. 73, s. 1, note 1, c corrected by hand to d in both D-brd: Rp and D-brd: F copies of '21.

[8] Amen, amen dico vobis

TEXT: John 6:54 (6:53)

Amen, amen dico vobis. Nisi manducaveritis carnem Filii hominis, et biberitis ejus sanguinem, non habebitis vitam in vobis.	Amen, amen, I say unto you: Except you eat the flesh of the Son of man, and drink his blood, you shall not have life in you.

SOURCE: *Corolla* (1621), 5

No commentary.

[9] Ecce Panis Angelorum

TEXT: Verse 21 of the Sequence "Lauda Sion," at Mass, Corpus Christi (altered)

Ecce Panis Angelorum, Factus cibus viatorum:	Behold, the Bread of Angels, made the food of wayfarers.

Vere Panis Angelorum,
Non mittendus canibus.

Truly the Bread of Angels, not to be cast to the dogs.

SOURCE: *Corolla* (1621), 6

COMMENTARY: M. 37, s. 2, note 2, c' corrected by hand to d'. M. 46, s. 1, note 4, g'.

[10] Adoro te supplex

TEXT: Verses 1, 4, and 7 of the Hymn for Corpus Christi attributed to St. Thomas Aquinas (altered)

Adoro te supplex,
  latens Deitas,
Quae sub his figuris
  vere latitas;
Tibi se cor meum
  totum subjicit,
Quia te contemplans,
  totum deficit.

Humbly I adore thee, concealed Deity, who hidest truly under these figures. My heart subjects itself entirely to thee, for in contemplating thee, it wholly fails.

Plagas, sicut Thomas,
  non intueor,
Deum tamen meum
  te confiteor,
Fac me tibi semper
  magis credere.
In te spem habere,
  te diligere.

I do not gaze at thy wounds as Thomas did, yet I confess that thou art my God. Make me ever more and more believe in thee, hope in thee, and choose thee.

O Jesu, quem vere
  nunc aspicio,
Quando fiet istud
  quod jam sitio,
Ut, te revelata
  cernens facie
Visu sim beatus
  tuae gloriae.

O Jesus, whom I now truly behold, when will that thing come to pass for which I now thirst? So that seeing thee with thy countenance unveiled, I may be happy in the vision of thy glory.

SOURCE: *Corolla* (1621), 7

COMMENTARY: M. 14, s. 2, note 3, *sum* (verse 3). M. 18, s. 2, note 2, *sum* (verse 3). M. 21, s. 4, this measure is followed by instruction "post trinam repetitionem finis" and a final measure.

[11] Regina caeli laetare

TEXT: Antiphon of the B. V. M., Ordinary of the Divine Office at Compline

Regina caeli laetare, alleluia:
Quia quem meruisti portare,
alleluia: Resurrexit, sicut
dixit, alleluia. Ora pro nobis
Deum, alleluia.

Queen of heaven, rejoice, alleluia. For he whom thou wert privileged to bear, alleluia, has risen, as he said, alleluia. Pray God for us, alleluia.

SOURCES: *Corolla* (1621), 21
  Viridarium (RISM 1627²), 46

COMMENTARY: T/C2 found in B partbook of '21. S. 4, the ♭ in the key sig. is lacking on the first staff in '21. S. 4, no barlines in '27, except as indicated below.

M. 1, all parts, time sig. is C in '27. Mm. 6–7, s. 1, *alleluia* in '21, with the first syllable on note 1 of m. 6 and the last three on notes 4–6 of m. 7; '27 has *laetare alleluia* here. M. 7, s. 4, this measure lacking entirely in '27. M. 8, s. 1, notes 1–2, first two syllables of *alleluia* on these two notes in '21. M. 14, all parts, time sig. is **3** in '21 and '27. Mm. 15–17, 24–26, 28–30, 35, s. 4, barline after each of these measures in '27. M. 18, s. 1, note 2 (thr. m. 20, note 1), *ij* in '27. M. 20, s. 1, note 2 (thr. m. 22), text written out in '27. Mm. 24–28, s. 1, text written out in '27. M. 26, s. 2, note 2 (thr. m. 28), text written out in '27. M. 27, s. 1, note 1, superfluous *ij* in '21. M. 32, s. 1, note 2 (thr. m. 34), *alleluia* in '27. M. 36, s. 2, note 2 (thr. m. 38, note 1), *alleluia* in '27. M. 38, all parts, time sig. is C in '27. M. 41, s. 2, notes 2–3, minim and semiminim, respectively, in '27. M. 42, s. 4, note 4, defective minim in '21. M. 43, s. 1, note 2 (thr. m. 47, note 1), text written out in '27, with underlay as given in this ed. M. 43, s. 2, notes 1–4, *alleluia* given on these four notes in '21. M. 43, s. 4, notes 1–2, semiminim and minim, respectively, in '27. M. 43, s. 4, note 4, semiminim in '21. M. 44, s. 1, note 2 (thr. m. 45, note 7), *ij* given three times (two extra, according to text underlay in this ed.) in '21. M. 44, s. 2, note 1 (thr. m. 45, note 3), *ij* given four times (three extra, according to text underlay in this ed.) in '21. M. 44, s. 2, note 1 (thr. m. 47, note 1), text written out in '27, with underlay as given in this ed. M. 46, s. 4, note 3, fig. 6 lacking in '27. M. 52, all parts, time sig. is **3** in '21 and '27. Mm. 53–54, 62–64, 66–67, s. 4, barline after each of these measures in '27. M. 62, s. 1, note 1 (thr. m. 66), text written out in '27. M. 64, s. 2, note 2 (thr. m. 66), text written out in '27. M. 65, s. 1, note 1, superfluous *ij* in '21. M. 68, s. 1, note 2 (thr. m. 70, note 1), text written out in '27. M. 69, s. 2 (thr. m. 72, note 1), *ij ij* in '27. M. 72, s. 2, note 2 (thr. m. 74, note 1), text written out in '27. M. 74, s. 1 (thr. m. 76), *ij* in '27. M. 77, s. 2 (thr. m. 78, note 1), text written out in '27. M. 78, s. 1 (thr. m. 81), text written out in '27, with underlay as given in this ed.

[12] Et vidi, et ecce

TEXT: Apoc. (Rev.) 14:1–2

Et vidi, et ecce Agnus stabat supra montem Sion, et cum eo centum quadraginta quatuor millia, habentes nomen ejus, et nomen Patris ejus scriptum in frontibus suis. Et audivi vocem de caelo, tanquam vocem aquarum multarum, et tanquam vocem tonitrui magni; et vocem, quam audivi, sicut citharoedorum citharizantium in citharis suis.

And I beheld, and lo a Lamb stood upon mount Sion, and with him an hundred forty-four thousand, having his name, and the name of his Father, written on their foreheads. And I heard a voice from heaven, as the noise of many waters, and as the voice of great thunder; and the voice which I heard, was as the voice of harpers, harping on their harps.

SOURCES: *Cantiones* (1609), 30 (T2 and T3 only)
  Prompt. mus. (RISM 1622²), 98

COMMENTARY: S. 5, no barlines (except as indicated below) in '22.

M. 4, s. 2, note 3 (thr. m. 5, note 2), *ij* in '22. M. 4, s. 3 (thr. m. 5, note 2), text written out in '22. M. 9, s. 2, note

3 (thr. m. 10, note 2), text written out in '22. M. 11, s. 2, note 3 (thr. m. 12, note 1), *ij* in '22. M. 12, s. 3, note 3 (thr. m. 13, note 2), *quatraginta* in '09. M. 16, s. 2, notes 5–7, *quaduor* in '09. M. 23, s. 2, notes 1–7, text written out in '22. M. 23, s. 3, note 3 (thr. m. 25), *ij* in '22. M. 35, all parts, time sig. is $\frac{3}{2}$ in '09 and '22. Mm. 35–44, s. 5, barline after each of these measures in '22. M. 42, s. 3, dotted breve in '09 and '22. M. 51, s. 2, notes 3–4, single semiminim in '09 and '22 (different text underlay in each source, changed in this ed.). M. 55, s. 2, *ij* in '22. Mm. 56–57, s. 2, text written out in '22.

[13] Deus meus

TEXT: Ps. 62:2–5 (63:1–4)

Deus meus, ad te de luce vigilo. Sitivit in te anima mea; quam multipliciter tibi caro mea! In terra deserta, invia et inaquosa, sic in sancto apparui tibi, ut viderem virtutem tuam et gloriam tuam. Quoniam melior est misericordia tua super vitas, labia mea laudabunt te. Sic benedicam te in vita mea; et in nomine tuo levabo manus meas.

My God, to thee do I watch at break of day. For thee my soul hath thirsted; for thee my flesh, O how many ways! In a desert land, where there is no way and no water: so in the sanctuary have I come before thee, to see thy power and thy glory. For thy mercy is better than lives: thee my lips shall praise. Thus will I bless thee all my life long: and in thy name I will lift up my hands.

SOURCES: *Cantiones* (1609), 31 (B1 and B2 only)
Prompt. mus. (RISM 1622²), 159

COMMENTARY: S. 5, no barlines in '22.
M. 3, s. 2, note 2, ♯ lacking in '22. M. 20, s. 2, note 6 (thr. m. 21, note 7), text written out in '22. M. 21, s. 2, note 8 (thr. m. 22, note 3), *ij* in '22. M. 26, s. 1, note 3, minim corrected by hand to semiminim (indicated in printed *corrigenda*) in '22. M. 31, s. 1, note 4, e' in '22. M. 35, s. 3, *ij* in '22. M. 36, s. 3, text written out in '22. M. 40, s. 2, note 2, ♯ lacking in '22. M. 44, all parts, time sig. is $\frac{3}{2}$ in '09 and '22. M. 50, s. 3, notes 1–2, ligature is ♭ in '09 and ♮ in '22. M. 62, s. 1, notes 5–6, *meo* in '22. M. 62, s. 2, notes 3–5, *ij* in '22. Mm. 62–63, s. 3, text written out in '22. M. 64, s. 3 (thr. m. 65, note 2), *ij* in '22. M. 65, s. 3, note 3 (thr. m. 67), text written out in '22.

[14] Duo Seraphim

TEXT: Responsory and Versicle after Lesson viii in Matins, Feast of the Most Holy Trinity

Duo Seraphim clamabant alter ad alterum: Sanctus, sanctus Dominus, Deus Sabaoth: Plena est omnis terra gloria ejus. Tres sunt qui testimonium dant in caelo: Pater, Verbum, et Spiritus Sanctus; et hi tres unum sunt. Sanctus, sanctus . . .

Two Seraphim cried to each other, ''Holy, holy is the Lord, God of hosts! All the earth is filled with his glory!'' There are three that bear witness in heaven: the Father, the Word, and the Holy Spirit; and these three are one. ''Holy, holy . . .''

SOURCES: *Siren* (RISM 1616¹), 44
Siren (RISM 1622³), 44
Prompt. mus. (RISM 1623²), 136

COMMENTARY: C/T, C/T, A indicated in all parts in '16 and '23 and in C1 and C2 in '22; A and Bg in '22 indicate C, C, A. S. 5, no barlines in '16, '22, and '23.
M. 1, s. 1, time sig. is C in '23. M. 6, s. 5, alto clef in '16, '22, and '23. M. 7, s. 2, note 3 (thr. m. 8, note 1), text underlay one beat later in '23. M. 8, s. 5, after note 2, bass clef in '16, '22, and '23. M. 11, s. 5, after note 1, alto clef in '16, '22, and '23. M. 13, s. 2, note 4 (thr. m. 14), *ij* in '23. M. 13, s. 5, note 3, semiminim in '16. M. 16, s. 2, note 3 (thr. m. 17), text written out in '23. M. 18, all parts, time sig. is 3 in '16, '22, and '23. M. 25, all parts, time sig. is 3 in '16, '22, and '23. M. 29, s. 5, note 2, fig. 6 in '16, '22, and '23 (meant to apply not to the note, but to its dot, and therefore placed under m. 30, note 1 in this ed.). M. 32, s. 2, note 3 (thr. m. 33, note 1), *ij* in '23. M. 32, s. 3, note 3 (thr. m. 33), *ij* in '23. M. 34, s. 1, notes 3–5, text written out in '22. M. 35, s. 1, *ij* in '22. M. 34, s. 5, note 1, a in '23. M. 34, s. 5, note 1, corrected from semiminim to minim in printed *corrigenda* of '23. M. 40, s. 1, note 4 (thr. m. 42), *ij* in '23. M. 45, s. 3, *caelis* in '16; *caelos* in '22. M. 57, s. 3, *ij* in '23. M. 58, all parts, time sig. is 3 in '16, '22, and '23. M. 59, s. 5, note 2, fig. 6 lacking in '16 and '22. M. 63, s. 1, note 4, text underlay of *-mnis terra* begins here in '23. M. 65, s. 2, note 3, e' corrected by hand to c' in '22. M. 65, s. 3, note 3 (thr. m. 66), text written out in '22. M. 67, s. 1, note 3 (thr. m. 68), *ij* in '23. M. 69, s. 1, text written out in '23. M. 69, s. 3, *ij* in '23. M. 70, s. 3 (thr. m. 71), text written out in '23. M. 70, s. 5, notes 4–5, fig. 6 lacking in '16 and '23, although '23 has two tied minims.

[15] Regi saeculorum immortali

TEXT: 1 Tim. 1:17

Regi saeculorum immortali, et invisibili, soli Deo, honor et gloria in saecula saeculorum. Amen.

To the King of ages, immortal and invisible, the only God, be honor and glory for ever and ever. Amen.

SOURCE: *Quercus* (1619), 1

COMMENTARY: M. 1, s. 3, ♭ in key sig. printed (incorrectly) on 3d line of staff. M. 8, s. 5, the barline after this measure is very faint. M. 13, s. 5, note 2, F♯. M. 20, s. 2, note 5, superfluous *ij*. M. 26, all parts, time sig. is 3. M. 30, s. 1, breve indicated as perfect by breve rest that follows (m. 31). M. 39, s. 1, rest barely visible.

[16] Nativitas tua

TEXT: Antiphon at Magnificat in 2d Vespers, Nativity of the Blessed Virgin

Nativitas tua, Sancta Dei Genitrix, gaudium annuntiavit in universo mundo: ex te enim ortus est Sol justitiae,

Thy birth, O holy Mother of God, heralded joy to all the world. For from thee has risen the Sun of justice, Christ our

Christus Deus noster: qui solvens maledictionem, dedit benedictionem: et confundens mortem, donavit nobis vitam sempiternam.

God, who, destroying the curse, gave blessing, and damning death, bestowed on us life everlasting.

SOURCES: *Quercus* (1619), 2
Prompt. mus. (RISM 1627[1]), 205

COMMENTARY: S. 5, no barlines in '27.

M. 1, all parts, time sig. is ₵ in '27. M. 10, s. 1 (thr. m. 11, note 1), text written out in '27. Mm. 18–19, s. 1, text written out in '27. Mm. 29 and 31–32, s. 2, copy of '19 in D-brd: Hs has different underlay of both examples of *Deus* in the text (this ed. follows version of '19 in D-brd: Rp). M. 29, s. 5, note 3, fig. 6 lacking in '27. M. 39, s. 2, note 3 (thr. m. 40), *ij* in '27. M. 45, s. 1, notes 1–5, text written out in '27. M. 45, s. 1, note 6 (thr. m. 46, note 4), *ij* in '27. M. 49, s. 5, note 3, fig. ♯ in '19 and '27. M. 52, s. 3, note 6, B♭ in '27. M. 54, s. 1, note 3 (thr. m. 56, note 1), text written out in '27.

[17] O beata ubera

TEXT: From the Responsory after Lesson vii in Matins, Nativity of Our Lord.

O beata ubera et beata viscera Mariae Virginis, quae portaverunt et lactaverunt aeterni Patris Filium.

O blessed breasts and blessed womb of the Virgin Mary, which bore and nursed the Son of the eternal Father.

SOURCES: *Quercus* (1619), 3
Viridarium (RISM 1627[2]), 95

COMMENTARY: S. 5, no barlines in '27.

M. 1, all parts, time sig. is ₵ in '27. M. 18, s. 5, note 3, fig. 6 lacking in '27. M. 20, s. 5, note 4, fig. ♯ in '27. M. 22, s. 2, notes 2–5, *portaveruūt* in '19. Mm. 23–24, s. 1, text written out in '27. Mm. 27–28, s. 3, *ij* in '27. M. 31, s. 1, note 5 (thr. m. 32), text written out in '27. M. 32, s. 5, note 1, A corrected by hand to B♭ in '19. M. 36, s. 5, note 1, fig. ♯ in '27.

[18] Salve, Regina

TEXT: Antiphon of the B. V. M., Ordinary of the Divine Office at Compline

Salve, Regina, mater misericordiae: Vita, dulcedo, et spes nostra, salve. Ad te clamamus, exsules, filii Hevae. Ad te suspiramus, gementes et flentes in hac lacrimarum valle. Eia ergo, Advocata nostra, illos tuos misericordes oculos ad nos converte. Et Jesum, benedictum fructum ventris tui, nobis post hoc exsilium ostende. O clemens: O pia: O dulcis Virgo Maria.

Hail, Queen, mother of mercy; our life, comfort, and hope—hail. To thee we cry, exiled sons of Eve; to thee we sigh, mourning and weeping in this vale of tears. Come, then, our advocate; turn thine eyes of mercy toward us. And after this exile, show us Jesus, the blessed fruit of thy womb. O gentle, O loving, O sweet Virgin Mary.

SOURCE: *Quercus* (1619), 4, 5

COMMENTARY: [Prima pars]—M. 31, s. 3, note 5, minim. M. 32, s. 3, note 1, minim. M. 34, s. 3, time sig. is ○ $\frac{3}{2}$; all other parts have **3**. M. 56, s. 1, semibreve corrected by hand to breve.

Secunda pars—M. 2, s. 5, note 1, fig. is 6 (corrected to ♭ in this ed.).

[19] Beatus vir

TEXT: Ecclus. 31:8–9

Beatus vir qui inventus est sine macula, et qui post aurum non abiit, nec speravit in pecuniae thesauris! Quis est hic? et laudabimus eum; fecit enim mirabilia in vita sua.

Blessed is the man that is found without blemish: and that hath not gone after gold, nor put his trust in treasures of money. Who is he? And we will praise him, for he hath done wonderful things in his life.

SOURCE: *Quercus* (1619), 6

COMMENTARY: M. 6, s. 5, note 5, semiminim. M. 13, s. 5, note 4, fig. has both ♭ and 6 (6 is moved to previous note in this ed.).

[20] Laetamini in Domino

TEXT: Ps. 31:11 (32:11)

Laetamini in Domino, et exsultate, justi; et gloriamini, omnes recti corde. Alleluia.

Be glad in the Lord, and rejoice, ye just, and glory, all ye right of heart. Alleluia.

SOURCE: *Quercus* (1619), 7

COMMENTARY: M. 31, s. 3, note 4, A. M. 40, s. 2, note 4, b♭'.

[21] Media nocte

TEXT: Matt. 25:6

Media nocte clamor factus est: Ecce sponsus venit, exite obviam ei. Alleluia.

At midnight there was a cry made: "Behold the bridegroom cometh, go ye forth to meet him." Alleluia.

SOURCE: *Quercus* (1619), 8

COMMENTARY: M. 2, s. 1, note the use of black notation ("nocte") here and in m. 3, s. 3; m. 5, s. 2; m. 6, s. 3; and m. 7, s. 1. M. 13, s. 5, note 3, f. M. 29, s. 3, note 6, superfluous *ij*. M. 34, s. 1, first word is *exise*. M. 45, s. 1, note 2, superfluous *ij*.

[22] In omnem terram

TEXT: Ps. 18:5 (19:4)

In omnem terram exivit sonus eorum, et in fines orbis terrae verba eorum.

Their sound hath gone forth into all the earth: and their words unto the ends of the world.

SOURCE: *Quercus* (1619), 9

COMMENTARY: M. 15, s. 5, note 2, c corrected by hand to d.

[23] Jesu nostra redemptio

TEXT: Verses 1 and 2 of Hymn for Corpus Christi and the Ascension of Our Lord

Jesu nostra redemptio,	Jesus, our redemption, love,
Amor et desiderium,	and desire, [God, creator of all
[Deus, creator omnium]*	things,] Man at the end of
Homo in fine temporum.	time. What kindness con-
Quae te vicit clementia,	quered thee that thou didst
Ut nostra ferres crimina,	bear our offences, suffering
Crudelem mortem patiens,	cruel death to raise us up from
Ut nos a morte tolleres!	death!

*This line not set by Aichinger.

SOURCE: *Quercus* (1619), 10

COMMENTARY: S. 1, "Sopra o leggiadri ochi." S. 2, 3, and 5, "Supra o leggiadri ochi."
   M. 7, all parts, double barline after this measure.

[24] Ave Regina caelorum

TEXT: Antiphon of the B. V. M., Ordinary of the Divine Office at Compline

Ave Regina caelorum,	Hail, Queen of heaven; hail,
Ave Domina Angelorum:	Mistress of the angels; hail,
Salve radix, salve porta,	root of Jesse; hail, gate
Ex qua mundo lux est orta:	through which the Light rose
Gaude Virgo gloriosa,	over the world. Rejoice, re-
Super omnes speciosa:	nowned Virgin, beautiful
Vale, o valde decora,	above all. Farewell, O exceed-
Et pro nobis Christum	ingly fine lady, and prevail
exora.	upon Christ for us.

SOURCES: *Quercus* (1619), 11
         Viridarium (RISM 1627²), 115

COMMENTARY: S. 5, no barlines in '27.
   M. 1, all parts, time sig. is ¢ in '27. M. 2, s. 5, bass clef in '19 and '27. M. 3, s. 2, note 3 (thr. m. 5, note 7), text written out in '27. Mm. 7–8, s. 2, text written out in '27. M. 8, s. 5, note 1, fig. ♯ plus 7 6 5 in '27. M. 9, s. 5, note 3, fig. ♯ plus 3 6 3 in '27. Mm. 15–16, note the unusual parallel fifths between the Bassus and thoroughbass (s. 3, 5), moving in unison, and the Altus (s. 1). M. 16, all parts, time sig. is 3 in '19 and '27. M. 17, s. 5, note 1, fig. ♯ in '27. M. 22, all parts, time sig. is ¢ in '27. M. 22, s. 5, note 4, fig. ♯ in '27. M. 25, s. 1, note 6, a in '27. M. 28, s. 3, note 6 (thr. m. 29, note 2), no indication of text in '27. Mm. 33–35, s. 3, *ij* in '27. Mm. 38–40, s. 1, text written out in '27.

[25] Justus ut palma florebit

TEXT: Ps. 91:13 (92:12)

Justus ut palma florebit; et sic-	The just shall flourish like the
ut cedrus Libani multiplicabi-tur.	palm tree: and he shall grow up like the cedar of Lebanon.

SOURCE: *Quercus* (1619), 12

COMMENTARY: M. 3, s. 5, note 3, fig. 6 one note later. M. 15, s. 3, note 5 (thr. m. 16, note 1), semibreve corrected by hand to breve. M. 17, s. 1, note 1 is dotted. M. 26, s. 2, note 3, cautionary ♯. M. 33, s. 1, note 4, fusa lacks flag. M. 33, s. 3, note 2, superfluous *ij*.

[26] Ecce sacerdos magnus

TEXT: Little Chapter at Lauds, Terce, and 2d Vespers, Common of a Confessor Bishop (incorporating Ecclus. 44:17)

Ecce sacerdos magnus, qui in diebus suis placuit Deo, et inventus est justus, et in tempore iracundiae factus est reconciliatio.	Behold a great priest, who in his days pleased God and was found just; and in the time of wrath he became a means of reconciliation.

SOURCE: *Quercus* (1619), 13

COMMENTARY: M. 14, s. 5, note 4, c. M. 27, s. 5, notes 1–2 tied, as shown in this ed. M. 30, all parts, time sig. is 3. M. 49, s. 2, note 4 (thr. m. 50, note 5), *reconeiliatio*.

[27] Hoc in templo

TEXT: Verse 3 of "Angularis fundamentum" (a continuation of "Urbs Jerusalem beata"), Hymn at Lauds and the Hours, Common of the Dedication of a Church

Hoc in templo, summe Deus,	In this temple, come, God
Exoratus adveni;	most high, won over by en-
Et clementi bonitate	treaties, and, with merciful
Precum vota suscipe;	goodness, receive our offer-
Largam benedictionem	ings of prayers. Thy abundant
Hic infunde jugiter.	blessing pour out continually in this place.

SOURCE: *Quercus* (1619), 14

COMMENTARY: M. 16, s. 2, note 2, g' corrected by hand to f' in D-brd: Rp copy. Mm. 52–53, s. 3, *precum vota suscipe*. Mm. 56–57, s. 3, *precum vota suscipe*.

[28] Ave, vivens hostia

TEXT: Verse 1 (slightly altered) of Hymn for Corpus Christi

Ave, vivens hostia,	Hail, living Host, truth, and
Veritas et vita,	life. Through thee all sac-
Per te sacrificia	rifices are ended. Through
Cuncta sunt finita,	thee the glory of the Father is
Per te patri gloria	given.
Datur infinita.	

SOURCE: *Corolla* (1621), 8

COMMENTARY: M. 17, all parts, time sig. is 3. M. 32, s. 5, note 1, fig. is 6. M. 34, s. 5, note 4, fig. is 6.

[29] Memoriam fecit

TEXT: Ps. 110:4–5 (111:4–5)

Memoriam fecit mirabilium suorum, misericors et miserator Dominus. Escam dedit timentibus se.

He hath made a remembrance of his wonderful works, being a merciful and gracious Lord: he hath given food to them that fear him.

SOURCE: *Corolla* (1621), 9

COMMENTARY: M. 20, all parts, time sig. is **3**. M. 27, s. 5, note 3, semibreve almost entirely black. M. 35, s. 1, note 1, cautionary ♯. M. 36, s. 5, note 1, dotted semibreve almost entirely black. M. 45, s. 5, note 2, semibreve almost entirely black. M. 57, all parts, time sig. is **3**. M. 72, s. 2, note 1, cautionary ♯. M. 87, s. 3, note 2, superfluous *ij*.

[30] O sacrum convivium!

TEXT: Antiphon at 2d Vespers in Corpus Christi

O sacrum convivium! in quo Christus sumitur: recolitur memoria passionis ejus: mens impletur gratia: et futurae gloriae nobis pignus datur.

O holy banquet, in which Christ is received, in which the memory of his passion is renewed, in which the soul is filled with grace and a pledge of future glory is given us.

SOURCE: *Corolla* (1621), 10

COMMENTARY: S. 2, ♭ printed as key sig. in every staff of partbook but crossed out by hand.
M. 28, all parts, time sig. is **3**. M. 35, s. 2 (thr. m. 36, note 1), *recolitut* corrected by hand to *recolitur*. M. 36, s. 1, note 1, semibreve almost entirely black in D-brd: Rp copy. M. 49, s. 3, note 2, semibreve almost entirely black.

[31] In nomine Jesu

TEXT: Introit at Mass, the Holy Name of Jesus (Phil. 2:10–11)

In nomine Jesu omne genu flectatur, caelestium, terrestrium et infernorum. Alleluia. Et omnis lingua confiteatur, quia Dominus noster Jesus Christus. Alleluia. In gloria est Dei Patris. Alleluia.

In the name of Jesus every knee should bow, of those that are in heaven, on earth, and under the earth. Alleluia. And every tongue should confess that our Lord Jesus Christ—Alleluia—is in the glory of God the Father. Alleluia.

SOURCE: *Philomela* (RISM 1624[1]), 41

COMMENTARY: M. 18, s. 2, time sig. is ○**3**; the other parts have **3**. Mm. 18–34, s. 5, partial text printed, evidently to serve as guide to organist. M. 33, all parts, time sig. is **3**. M. 41, all parts, time sig. is **3**.

[32] Quem terra, pontus, aethera

TEXT: Verses 1, 2, and 4 of the Hymn at Matins, along with verse 3 of "O gloriosa Virginum," Hymn at Lauds, both of the Common of Feasts of the B. V. M.; the refrain is based on verse 1 of the Hymn in the Litany of Loreto

Quem terra, pontus, aethera
Colunt, adorant, praedicant,
Trinam regentem machinam,
Claustrum Mariae bajulat.
   Maria Mater gratiae,
   Mater misericordiae,
   Tu nos ab hoste protege,
   In hora mortis suscipe.

The womb of Mary carries him who rules the threefold fabric, and whom the earth, sea, and heaven honor, worship, and praise. Mary, Mother of grace, Mother of mercy, protect us from the enemy, and receive us at the hour of death.

Cui luna, sol et omnia
Deserviunt per tempora,
Perfusa caeli gratia,
Gestant puellae viscera.
   Maria Mater gratiae,
· · · · · · · · · ·

The Maiden's womb, filled with the grace of heaven, bears him to whom the moon, sun, and all things are subject, each in its time. Mary, Mother of grace . . .

Beata caeli nuntio,
Fecunda Sancto Spiritu,
Desideratus gentibus
Cujus per alvum fusus est.
   Maria Mater gratiae,
· · · · · · · · · ·

Filled with joy by the message from heaven and made fruitful by the Holy Spirit, through her womb was brought forth the Desired of nations. Mary, Mother of grace . . .

Tu Regis alti janua
Et porta lucis fulgida:
Vitam datam per Virginem,
Gentes redemptae, plaudite.
   Maria Mater gratiae,
· · · · · · · · · ·

Thou art the door for the great King and the shining palace for the light. Rejoice, ransomed nations, in the life given by the Virgin. Mary, Mother of grace . . .

SOURCES: *Cantiones* (1609), 32 (T and B only)
Viridarium (RISM 1627[2]), 185

COMMENTARY: S. 6, no barlines in '27.
M. 2, s. 6, bass clef in '27. Mm. 16–19, s. 4, text written out in '27. M. 20, all parts, time sig. is $\frac{3}{2}$ in '09 and '27. M. 30, s. 1–4, note 1, & in '27. M. 32, s. 4, dot after note 1 in '09. M. 49, s. 2, time sig. is (incorrect) $\frac{2}{2}$ in '27; all remaining parts in '09 and '27 have $\frac{3}{2}$. M. 59, s. 1–4, note 1, & in '27. M. 79, s. 6, note 4, an extra semiminim B in '27. M. 81, all parts, time sig. is $\frac{3}{2}$ in '09 and '27. M. 91, s. 1–4, note 1, & in '27. M. 100, s. 3, note 2 (thr. m. 101, note 1), *ij* in '27. M. 105, s. 3 (thr. m. 107, note 1), *gentes redemptae plaudite* in '27. M. 107, s. 3, note 2 (thr. m. 112), *ij ij* in '27. M. 108, s. 6, note 3, cautionary ♯ in '27. M. 111, s. 6, note 4, d in '27. M. 113, all parts, time sig. is $\frac{3}{2}$ in '09 and '27. M. 114, s. 6, note 1 dotted in '27. M. 123, s. 1–4, note 1, & in '27. M. 126, s. 3, time sig. is (incorrect) ¢ in '27. M. 126, s. 1–3, note 2, & in '27. M. 126, s. 4, note 2, *et* in '27. M. 128, s. 1, note 2, & in '27. M. 128, s. 3, note 2 (thr. m. 129, note 2), *ij* in '27. M. 128, s. 4, note 5 (thr. m. 129, note 2), *ij* in '27.

[33] Angelus sanctae Gabriel Mariae

TEXT: Source unidentified

Angelus sanctae
Gabriel Mariae,
Luce cadentes
Humeros amictus

The Angel Gabriel, surrounded with light on his dazzling shoulders, announces the birth to holy Mary. The

Nunciat partum; Trepida rubescunt Ora puellae.	trembling countenance of the girl grows red.
Quid times virgo? Deus ipse tecum, Sponsa tu Regis; Fluet aura sancti Spiritus in te Facietque pulchra Prole parentem.	"What dost thou fear, Virgin? God himself is with thee; thou art bride of the King. The breath of the Holy Spirit will flow into thee and will make thee a mother with noble off-spring."
Ecce me Regis Famulam superni; Nil moror; quicquid Jubet ille fiat; Mox gravescentis Sacra vis per alvi Funditur artus.	"Behold me, the handmaiden of the King on high. I do not object. Let whatever he commands be done." Soon, the sacred power is spread throughout the veins of the pregnant womb.
Jam novo tellus Juvenescit aevo, Jam fides et pax Superum; favorque Priscus abjectos Miserae nepotes Respicit Evae.	Already the earth is regaining strength in a new age. Now there is faith and peace with heaven; and the ancient favor considers the miserable descendants of wretched Eve.
Gaudium cunctis Hodie Maria Angelis fecit; Reseravit uno Verbulo coelum; Stetit acta nostrae Causa salutis.	Today Mary gave joy to all the angels. She unlocked heaven with one little word; the cause of our salvation, having been performed, stood firm.
Sint tibi laudes Quia credidisti Mater aeternae Benedictionis; Te salutamus Veniente sole Teque cadente.	Let praises be unto thee, Mother of eternal blessing, because thou didst believe. We greet thee when the sun rises and when it sets.

SOURCE: *Encomium* (1617), [3]

COMMENTARY: Prima pars—C1, C2, T, and B have heading: "Sopra il aria ortensia"; B has, in addition: "Hic requiritur necessariò Bassus generalis."

Secunda pars—M. 3, s. 1, note 4 (thr. m. 5, note 1), *superin.* M. 7, s. 6, note 2, fig. 6 (possibly meant to apply to dot after previous note, but more likely meant to be a ♭ altering the note itself, as realized in this ed.). M. 24, s. 2, note 5, ♯ for this note printed at left of the next note.

Tertia pars—M. 3, s. 3, note 3, cautionary ♯. M. 17, s. 6, note 2, F. Mm. 19–20, s. 2, *subjectos.*

Quarta pars—M. 4, s. 6, tenor clef. M. 6, s. 6, bass clef. M. 12, s. 1, note 2, c". M. 21, s. 6, note 1, fig. 6 belonging with this note (as given in this ed.) is printed over the next note (along with the fig. ♯ pertaining to that note).

Quinta et ultima pars—M. 16, s. 1, note 2, bb'. M. 19, s. 1 and 3, note the evidently intended parallel unisons here and in m. 27. M. 20, s. 4, time sig. is ₵³₂ remaining parts have **3**.

[34] Angelus Domini descendit

TEXT: Matt. 28:2, 5, 6 (altered)

Angelus Domini descendit de caelo, et accedens revolvit lapidem, seditque super eam, dixitque mulieribus: Nolite timere: scio enim, quia crucifixum, quaeritis. Jam surrexit: venite, et videte locum ubi positus erat Dominus. Alleluia.	An angel of the Lord descended from heaven, and coming, rolled back the stone, and sat upon it, and said to the women: "Fear not, for I know that you seek him who was crucified. He is already risen; come, and see the place where the Lord was laid." Alleluia.

SOURCE: *Flores* (1626), 11

COMMENTARY: S. 1, printed in C partbook with heading: "5. voc. Symphonia 2. Violini Temp. Pasch. Cantus." S. 2, this part missing and therefore completely editorial in this ed. S. 3, printed in A partbook with heading: "Concerto à 5. con una Simphon. di 2. Violini. Temp. pasch. Altus." S. 4, 5, and 7, headings similar to the preceding (with different part names). S. 7, no barlines.

M. 9, all parts, time sig. is **3**. M. 31, s. 5, note 3, d. M. 37, all parts, time sig. is **3**. M. 52, s. 7, note 1, dot lacking. M. 69, s. 1, note 1 has ♯. M. 73, s. 1–5, barline after this measure. M. 80, s. 7, head of note 1 completely splotched with ink. M. 87, all parts, time sig. is **3**. M. 87, s. 7, after time sig., tenor clef. M. 88, s. 7, bass clef. M. 100, s. 3 (thr. m. 106, note 1), the three abbreviations (*alle., all.,* and *all.*) begin on m. 101, note 1; m. 103, note 2; and m. 104, note 1, respectively.

[35] Paratum cor meum

TEXT: Ps. 107:2–6, 14 (108:1–5,13)

Paratum cor meum, Deus, paratum cor meum; cantabo, et psallam tibi in gloria mea. Exsurge, gloria mea; exsurge, psalterium et cithara; exsurgam diluculo, et confitebor tibi in populis, Domine, et psallam tibi in nationibus; quia magna est super caelos misericordia tua, et usque ad nubes veritas tua. Exaltare super caelos, Deus, et super omnem terram gloria tua. In Deo faciemus virtutem; et ipse ad nihilum deducet inimicos nostros. Alleluia.	My heart is ready, O God, my heart is ready: I will sing and give praise to thee with my glory. Arise, my glory; arise, psaltery and harp: I will arise in the morning early; and I will praise thee, O Lord, among the people: and I will sing unto thee among the nations. For thy mercy is great above the heavens: and thy truth even unto the clouds. Be thou exalted, O God, above the heavens, and thy glory over all the earth. Through God we shall do mightily: and he will bring our enemies to nothing. Alleluia.

SOURCE: *Flores* (1626), 12

COMMENTARY: S. 1, printed in C partbook with heading: "Symphonia 2. Violini. 5. voc. Cantus." S. 2, this part missing and therefore completely editorial in this ed. S. 3, printed in A partbook with heading: "Concerto à 5. con una Symphon. di 2. Violini. Cantus." S. 4, 5, and 7, headings identical to the preceding (with different part names). S. 7, no barlines.

M. 13, s. 5, *spallam*.   M. 17, s. 1, 4, and 5, time sig. is $\phi\frac{3}{2}$; s. 3 has $\text{¢}\frac{3}{2}$; and s. 7 has **3**.   M. 49, s. 7, superfluous semiminim b♭ between notes 7 and 8.   M. 51, s. 1, 5, and 7, time sig. is **3**; s. 3 and 4 have $\text{¢}\frac{3}{2}$.   M. 55, s. 3, note 1, g'.   M. 81, s. 7, tenor clef.   M. 82, s. 7, after note 3, bass clef.   M. 83, s. 7, note 2, fig. 6 printed over next note.   M. 85, s. 4, notes 3–5, *gloriam*.   M. 89, s. 1, 5, and 7, time sig. is **3**; s. 3 has $\phi\frac{3}{2}$; and s. 4 has $\text{¢}\frac{3}{2}$.   M. 118, all parts, time sig. is **3**.   M. 118, s. 1, note 4, minim.   M. 118, s. 7, after time sig., tenor clef.   M. 122, s. 7, bass clef.   M. 133, s. 7, note 2, fig. 6 printed above previous note.

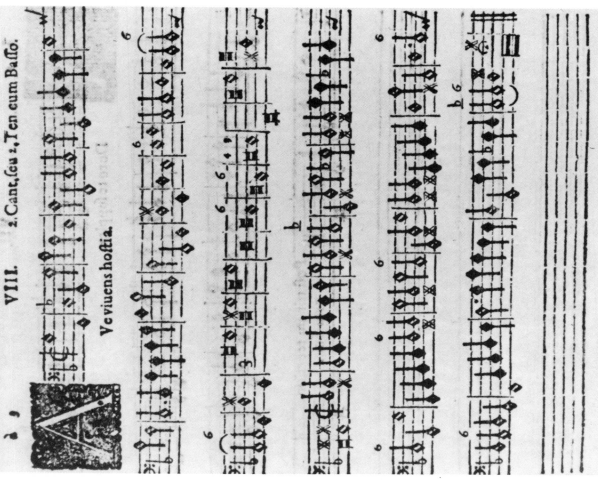

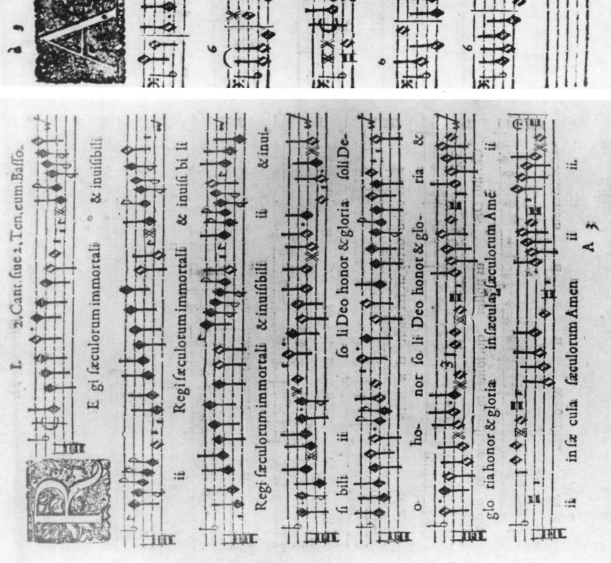

Plate I. Gregor Aichinger, *Quercus Dodonaea* (Augsburg: Johann Praetorius, 1619), Cantus I, no. 1, "Regi saeculorum immortali", (no. [15] in this edition). Proskesche Musikbibliothek (Bischöfliche Zentralbibliothek), Regensburg. (Microfilm supplied through the Deutsches Musikgeschichtliches Archiv, Kassel)

Plate II. Gregor Aichinger, *Corolla eucharistica* (Augsburg: Johann Praetorius, 1621), Bassus generalis, no. 8, "Ave, vivens hostia" (no. [28] in this edition). Proskesche Musikbibliothek (Bischöfliche Zentralbibliothek), Regensburg. (Microfilm supplied through the Deutsches Musikgeschichtliches Archiv, Kassel)

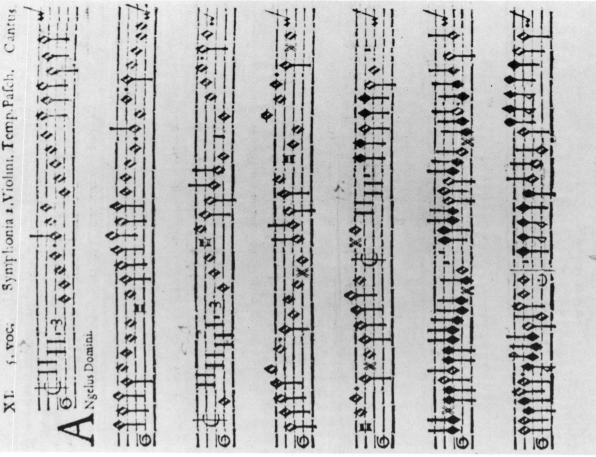

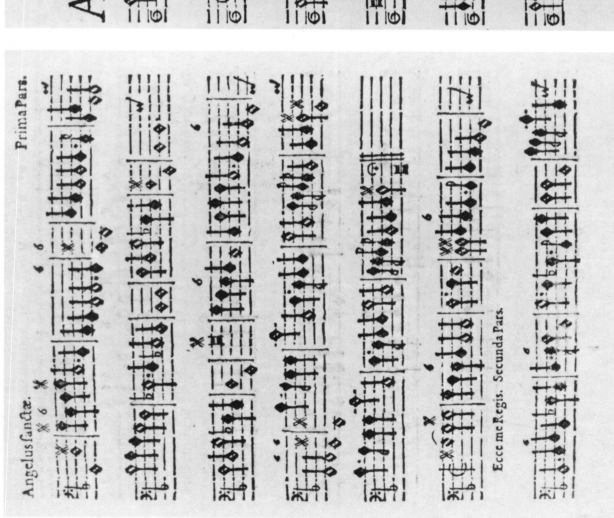

Plate III. Gregor Aichinger, *Encomium verbo incarnato* (Ingolstadt: Gregor Hänlin, 1617), Bassus generalis, beginning of "Angelus sanctae Gabriel Mariae" (no. [33] in this edition). Proskesche Musikbibliothek (Bischöfliche Zentralbibliothek), Regensburg. (Microfilm supplied through the Deutsches Musikgeschichtliches Archiv, Kassel)

Plate IV. Gregor Aichinger, *Flores musici* (Augsburg: Johann Ulrich Schönigk, 1626), Cantus (Violino I), beginning of no. 11, "Angelus Domini descendit" (no. [34] in this edition). Proskesche Musikbibliothek (Bischöfliche Zentralbibliothek), Regensburg. (Microfilm supplied through the Deutsches Musikgeschichtliches Archiv, Kassel)

[1] Mirabile mysterium

Mi- ra- bi- le my- ste- ri-um, mi- ra- bi- le, ⟨mi-

Mi- ra- bi- le my- ste- ri-um, mi- ra- bi-

-ra- bi- le⟩ my- ste- ri- um de- cla- ra-

- le my- ste- ri- um de- cla- ra-

- tur ho- di- e: in-no-van-tur na- tu-

- tur ho- di- e: in-no- van-tur na- tu-

-psit; non com-mix-ti- o- nem pas- sus, nec_____ di- vi-

-rat as-sum- psit; non com-mix-ti- o- nem pas- sus, nec di-

-si- o- - nem. Al- le-lu- ia, ⟨al- le-

-vi- si- o- nem. Al- le-lu- ia, ⟨al- le- lu- ia,⟩

- lu- ia,⟩ al- le-lu- ia,_____ al- le- - lu-

al- le-lu- ia,_____ ⟨al- le- - lu-

6

[2] Angelus Domini

10

[3] Adorna thalamum tuum

Altus I

A- dor- na, ⟨a- dor- na⟩ tha- la- mum tu-

Altus II

A- dor- na, ⟨a- dor- na⟩ tha- la-

Bassus generalis

- um, Si- on, a- dor- na,

-mum tu- - um, Si- on, a- dor- na, ⟨a- dor- na⟩

⟨a- dor- na⟩ tha- la-mum tu- - um, Si- on,

tha- la-mum tu- - um, Si- - on, et sus- ci-

[4] Hic est panis

[5] Domine, non sum dignus

[6] Discubuit Jesus

Tenor I (Cantus I): Di- scu- bu- it Je- sus cum di- sci- pu- lis su- is, cum di- sci- pu- lis su- is, ⟨cum di- sci- pu- lis su- is.⟩ Et a- it, ⟨et a- it:⟩ De- si- de- ri- o de-

Tenor II (Cantus II): Di- scu- bu- it Je- sus cum di- sci- pu- lis su- is, cum di- sci- pu- lis su- is. Et a- it, ⟨et a- it:⟩ De- si- de- ri-

Bassus generalis

-si- de- ra- vi hoc pa- scha man-du- ca- re vo- bis- cum, de- si-

-o de- si- de- ra- vi hoc pa- scha man- du- ca- re vo- bis- cum,

-de- ri- o de- si- de- ra- vi hoc pa- scha man-du- ca- re vo- bis- cum,

de- si- de- ri- o de- si- de- ra- vi hoc pa- scha man-du- ca- re vo- bis- cum,

de- si- de- ri- o de- si- de- ra- vi hoc pa- scha man-du- ca-

⟨de- si- de- ri- o de- si- de- ra- vi⟩ hoc pa- scha man-du- ca- re vo-

[7] Caro mea

*This part was added by Johann Donfrid (1627). See Preface and Critical Notes.

vi- vet in ae- ter- num, qui man-

pa- nem, ⟨vi- vet in ae- ter- num,⟩ qui man- du- cat hunc

pa- nem, vi- vet in ae- ter- num,⟩ qui man- du- cat hunc

-du- cat hunc pa- nem, vi- vet in ae- ter- num.

pa- nem, vi- vet in ae- ter- num, in ae- ter- num.

pa- nem, vi- vet in ae- ter- num, in ae- ter- num.

[8] Amen, amen dico vobis

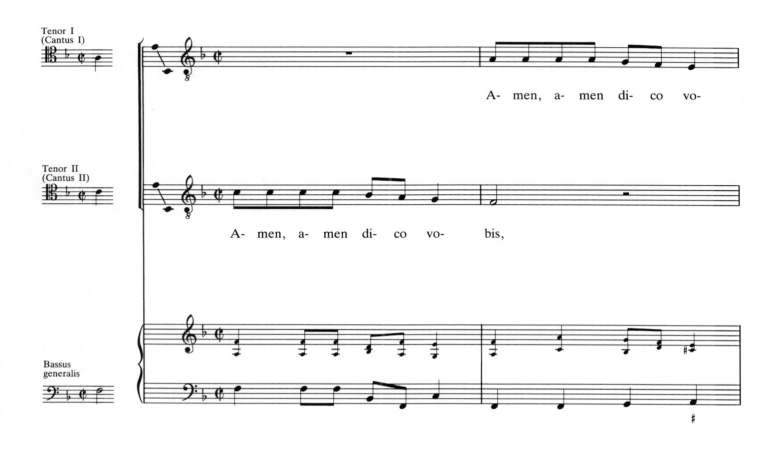

Tenor I (Cantus I): A- men, a- men di- co vo-

Tenor II (Cantus II): A- men, a- men di- co vo- bis,

Bassus generalis

-bis, ⟨a- men, a- men di- co vo- bis, a- men, a- men di- co vo-

⟨a- men, a- men di- co vo- bis, a- men, a- men di- co vo-

[9] Ecce Panis Angelorum

[10] Adoro te supplex

Tenor I (Cantus I)

A- do- ro te _____ sup- plex, la- tens De- i-
Pla- gas, sic- ut _____ Tho- mas, non in- tu- e-
O Je- su, quem _____ ve- re nunc a- spi- ci-

Tenor II (Cantus II)

A- do- ro te _____ sup- plex, la- tens De- i-
Pla- gas, sic- ut _____ Tho- mas, non _____ in- tu- e-
O Je- su, quem _____ ve- re nunc _____ a- spi- ci-

Bassus generalis

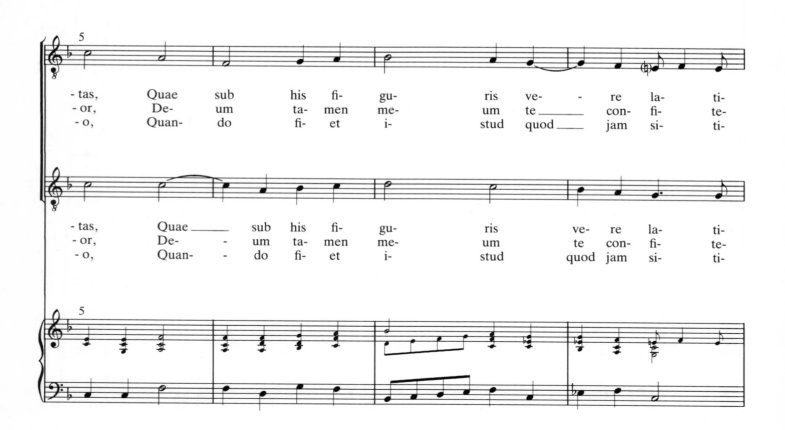

- tas, Quae sub his fi- gu- ris ve- re la- ti-
- or, De- um ta- men me- um te _____ con- fi- te-
- o, Quan- do fi- et i- stud quod _____ jam si- ti-

- tas, Quae _____ sub his fi- gu- ris ve- re la- ti-
- or, De- um ta- men me- um te con- fi- te-
- o, Quan- do fi- et i- stud quod jam si- ti-

[11] Regina caeli laetare

- ia, al- le- lu- ia, al- le- - lu- ia,

al- le- lu- ia, ⟨al- le- lu- ia, al- le- lu- ia,⟩

al- le- lu- ia, al- le- lu- ia, al- le- lu- ia,⟩

al- le- lu- ia, al- le- lu- ia, ⟨al- le- lu-

al- le- lu- ia, ⟨al- le- - lu- ia.⟩

- ia, al- le- lu- ia, al- le- lu- ia, al- le- lu- ia.⟩

[12] Et vidi, et ecce

46

48

[13] Deus meus

52

[14] Duo Seraphim

60

[15] Regi saeculorum immortali

Cantus I
(Tenor I)

Regi saeculorum immortali,

Cantus II
(Tenor II)

Regi saecu-

Bassus

Regi

Bassus
generalis

et invisibili, ⟨et invisibi-
-lorum immortali, et invisibili,
saeculorum immortali, et

5

-li,⟩ Regi saeculorum
⟨et invisibili,⟩ Regi saecu-
invisibili,

5

62

[16] Nativitas tua

Cantus I
(Tenor I)

Na- ti- vi- tas tu- a, ⟨na-

Cantus II
(Tenor II)

Na- ti- vi- tas tu- a,

Bassus

San-cta De- i Ge- ni- trix,

Bassus
generalis

-ti- vi- tas tu- a,⟩ San-cta De- i Ge- ni-trix,

San-cta De- i Ge- ni- trix, ⟨San-cta De- i Ge-ni-trix,⟩ na- ti- vi- tas tu-

na- ti- vi- tas tu- a, San-cta De- i Ge-ni-

65

[17] O beata ubera

72

[18] Salve, Regina

80

[19] Beatus vir

Cantus I
(Tenor I)

Be- a- - tus vir qui in- ven- tus est, ⟨qui in-

Cantus II
(Tenor II)

Be- a- tus vir qui in- ven- tus est, ⟨qui in-

Bassus

Be- a- tus vir qui in- ven- tus est, qui in-

Bassus
generalis

6   6

5

-ven- tus est⟩   si-ne ma- cu- la, ⟨si-ne ma- cu- la,⟩ et

-ven- tus est⟩ si-ne ma- cu- la, ⟨si-ne ma- cu- la,⟩ et qui post

-ven- tus est si-ne ma- cu- la, ⟨si-ne ma- cu- la,⟩ et qui post

5

84

[20] Laetamini in Domino

[21] Media nocte

[22] In omnem terram

[23] Jesu nostra redemptio

Cantus I
(Tenor I)

Cantus II
(Tenor II)

Bassus

Bassus
generalis

Je- su no- stra re- dem- pti- o, A- mor et de-

Je- su no- stra re- dem- pti- o, A- mor et de-

Je- su no- stra re- dem- pti- o, A- mor et de-

-si- de- ri- um, Ho- mo in fi- ne tem- po- rum. Quae te

-si- de- ri- um, Ho- mo in fi- ne tem- po- rum.

-si- de- ri- um, Ho- mo in fi- ne tem- po- rum.

[24] Ave Regina caelorum

[25] Justus ut palma florebit

[26] Ecce sacerdos magnus

Tenor I

Ec- - ce sa-cer- dos ma- gnus,

Tenor II

Ec- ce sa-cer-dos ma- gnus, ⟨ec- ce sa- cer- dos ma-

Bassus

Ec- ce sa-cer-dos ma- gnus, qui in di- e- bus

Bassus generalis

⟨ec- - ce sa-cer- dos_____ ma- gnus,⟩ qui in di- e- bus su-

- gnus,⟩ ec- ce sa- cer- dos ma- gnus,

su- is, ⟨qui in di- e- bus su-

[27] Hoc in templo

113

114

[28] Ave, vivens hostia

120

[29] Memoriam fecit

- men- ti-bus se,⟩ ti-

se, e- scam de- dit ti- men- ti- bus se,

e- scam de- dit ti- men- ti- bus se, ti- men- ti- bus se,

6

- men- ti-bus se, ⟨ti- men- ti-bus se,⟩ ti- men-ti- bus se.

ti- men-ti-bus se, ⟨ti- men- ti-bus se,⟩ ti- men-ti- bus se.

⟨ti- men- ti-bus se, ti- men-ti- bus se.⟩

[30] O sacrum convivium!

[31] In nomine Jesu

134

[32] Quem terra, pontus, aethera

Ma- ri- a Ma- ter gra- ti-ae, Ma- ter mi- se- ri- cor- di-ae, Tu nos ab ho-

Ma- ri- a Ma- ter gra- ti-ae, Ma- ter mi- se- ri- cor- di-ae, Tu nos ab ho-

Ma- ri- a Ma- ter gra- ti-ae, Ma- ter mi- se- ri- cor- di-ae, Tu nos ab ho-

Ma- ri- a Ma- ter gra- ti-ae, Ma- ter mi- se- ri- cor- di-ae, Tu nos ab ho-

-ste pro- te- ge, In ho- ra mor- tis sus- ci- pe. Cui lu- na, sol et

-ste pro- te- ge, In ho- ra mor- tis sus- ci- pe.

-ste pro- te- ge, In ho- ra mor- tis sus- ci- pe. Cu- i lu- na, sol et

-ste pro- te- ge, In ho- ra mor- tis sus- ci- pe.

[33] Angelus sanctae Gabriel Mariae

Tre- pi- da ru- be- scunt,

Tre- pi- da ru- be- scunt, tre- pi- da ru- be- scunt,

Tre- pi- da ru- be- scunt, ⟨tre- pi- da ru- be-

Tre- pi- da ru- be- scunt, tre- pi- da ru-

⟨tre- pi- da ru- be- scunt⟩ O- ra pu- el- lae.

⟨tre- pi- da ru- be- scunt⟩ O- ra pu- el- lae.

- scunt,⟩ tre- pi- da ru- be- scunt O- ra pu- el- lae. Tre- pi- da ru-

- be- scunt O- ra pu- el- lae.

Flu-et au- ra san- cti Spi- ri-tus in_____ te   Fa- ci-

Flu-et au- ra san- cti Spi- ri-tus in   te   Fa- ci- et-que pul- chra, ⟨fa- ci-

Fa- ci-et-que   pul-   chra Pro- le pa-

Fa- ci-et-que   pul- chra, ⟨fa-   ci-et-que

6   6   #6

- et- que pul- chra Pro-   - le pa-ren- tem.   Fa-   ci- et- que pul-

- et- que pul- chra⟩   Pro-   - le pa-ren- tem.

- ren-   tem,   pro-   le pa- ren- tem.   Fa- ci- et- que   pul-

pul-   chra⟩ Pro-   le pa- ren- tem.   Fa- ci- et- que pul-   chra,

- chra, ⟨fa- ci- et- que pul- chra⟩ Pro- le pa- ren- tem.

Fa- ci- et- que pul- chra Pro- le pa- ren- tem.

- chra Pro- le pa- ren- tem, pro- le pa- ren- tem.

⟨fa- ci- et- que pul- chra⟩ Pro- le pa- ren- tem.

Cantus I

Cantus II

Tenor

Bassus

Bassus generalis

Secunda pars

Ec- ce, ec- ce me Re- gis Fa- mu-lam su- per-

Ec- - ce me Re- gis Fa- mu-lam su- per-

Ec- ce, ec- ce me Re- gis Fa- mu-lam su- per-

154

⟨Mi- se- rae _____ ne- po- tes Re- spi- cit E- vae.⟩

Mi- se- rae _____ ne- po- tes Re- spi- cit E- vae.

⟨Mi- se- rae ne- po- tes Re- spi- cit E- vae.⟩

Mi- se- rae ne- po- tes Re- spi- cit E- vae.

Cantus I

Cantus II

Tenor

Bassus

Bassus generalis

Quarta pars

Gau- di- um cun- ctis Ho- di- e Ma- ri- a An-

163

166

Te sa- lu- ta- mus, ⟨te sa- lu- ta- mus⟩

Te sa- lu- ta- mus, ⟨te sa- lu- ta- mus⟩

Te sa- lu- ta- mus

Te sa- lu- ta- mus

Ve- ni-en- te so- le, ⟨ve- ni-en- te so- le⟩ Te-que ca- den- te.

Ve- ni-en- te so- le, ⟨ve- ni-en- te so- le⟩ Te- que ca- den- te.

Ve- ni-en- te so- le Te- que ca- den- te, te- que ca- den- te.

Ve- ni-en- te so- le, ve- ni-en- te so- le Te-que ca- den- te.

[34] Angelus Domini descendit

An- ge-lus Do- mi-ni de-scen-dit de cae- lo,

An- ge-lus Do- mi- ni de-scen-dit de cae-lo, _____ de cae-

* This part is missing in the source (1626) and was reconstructed by the editor.

170

- lo,

No- li- - te ti- me- re, no- li- te ti- me-

No- li- te ti- me- re, no- li- te ti- me-

Jam sur- re- xit: ve- ni- te, jam sur- re- xit: ve- ni- te,

Jam sur- re- xit: ve- ni- te, jam sur- re- xit: ve- ni- te, ⟨jam sur-

Jam sur- re- xit: ve- ni- te, jam sur- re- xit: ve- ni- te,

et vi- de- te lo- cum, ⟨et vi- de- te

-re- xit: ve- ni- te,⟩ et vi- de- te lo- cum

et vi- de- te lo- cum, ⟨et vi- de- te

lo- cum⟩ u- bi po- si- tus e- rat Do- mi- nus, u- bi

u- bi po- si- tus e- rat Do- mi- nus, u- bi

lo- cum⟩ u- bi po- si- tus e- rat Do- mi- nus,

po- si- tus e- rat, u- bi po- si- tus e- rat Do- mi- nus.

po- si- tus e- rat Do- mi- nus.

u- bi po- si- tus e- rat Do- mi- nus.

Al- le- - lu- ia, ⟨al- le- lu- ia,⟩ al- le- [lu- ia], ⟨al-

Al- le- lu- ia, al- l[e- - lu- ia], al- le- lu- ia, ___ al-

Al- le- lu- ia, ⟨al- le- lu- ia,⟩ al- le- lu- ia, ⟨al-

[35] Paratum cor meum

Pa- ra- tum cor me- um, De- us, pa- ra- tum cor

me- um, pa- ra- tum _____ cor me- um; can- ta-

can- ta- - bo, et

can- ta- - bo, et

* This part is missing in the source (1626) and was reconstructed by the editor.

et psal- lam ti- - bi in na- ti- o- ni- bus;

in na- ti- o- ni- bus;

et psal- lam ti- bi in na- ti- o- ni- bus;

qui- a ma- gna est su- - per cae- - los

mi- se- ri-

qui- - a ma- gna est su- per cae- los

et su-per o-mnem ter- ram, ⟨et su-per o-mnem ter- ram⟩

-los, De- us, et su-per o-mnem ter- ram, et su-per o-mnem ter- ram glo- ri- a

et su-per o-mnem ter- ram, ⟨et su-per o-mnem ter- ram⟩

glo- ri- a tu- a, glo- ri- a tu- a.

tu- a, glo- -ri- a tu- a.

glo- ri- a tu- a, _____ ⟨glo- -ri- a tu- a.⟩

In De- o fa- ci- e- mus vir- tu-

In De- o

In De- o fa- ci-